"A compellingly candid story! Not argument or ideology but data—first-person facts and utterly honest feelings." **PETER KREEFT**—Author, *Three Approaches to Abortion*

"As a founder of the National Coalition for Life and Choice, I have always encouraged people on both sides of the 'life line' to listen to and understand each other, though they may never agree. Abby Johnson's sincere and thoughtful story has much to teach both sides."

FREDERICA MATHEWES-GREEN—Author, *Real Choices: Listening to Women, Looking for Alternatives to Abortion,* www.frederica.com

"I'm grateful to Abby Johnson for having the courage to tell her story as a former director of a Planned Parenthood clinic in *Unplanned*. Though Planned Parenthood provides other services for women, it is the largest abortion provider in America. In this unique and compelling book, Abby shows the compassionate hearts of some of her coworkers, takes responsibility for her own participation in abortions, and shares the journey of how God in his grace and mercy delivered her from blindness. I hope that by reading this story you will be moved to do what you can to offer help and resources to women in need of them, and lovingly tell them the truth about their unborn child."

RANDY ALCORN—Author, *ProLife Answers to ProChoice Arguments* and *Why Pro-Life?*

"Abby's story is one of great moral courage in an age that groans for lack of it. Hers is a modern parable of hope for us all, witnessing to the truth that sets the human heart free. A riveting story." **MARJORIE DANNENFELSER**—President, Susan B. Anthony List

"Abby's gripping story gives a rare glimpse into the heart that motivates both pro-abortion and pro-life activities. Her book is a refreshing affirmation of the power of truth, which overcomes even the thickest deceptions. Abby's compelling experience gives invaluable insight both to those involved in providing abortion and those who struggle to see life triumph."

DONNA J. HARRISON, M.D.—President, American Association of Pro-Life Obstetricians and Gynecologists

"*Unplanned* is a powerful and compelling testimony of the power of prayer and love. A story of courage, conviction, and conversion, the book will draw you into Abby's life and her journey as her eyes are opened to the truth."

DR. ALVEDA C. KING—Pastoral Associate, Priests for Life; Founder, King for America; Niece of Dr. Martin Luther King, Jr.

"Think love and kindness can't make a difference in the abortion debate? Read Abby Johnson's story and find out how a pro-life ministry's peaceful and respectful witness forever changed the heart of this former Planned Parenthood clinic director."

JIM DALY—President, Focus on the Family

"Abby understands how good people can be misled, as she was, to support abortion under the guise of helping women. This is the remarkable story of how one director of a Planned Parenthood clinic came to realize the truth about abortion—and what she did about it." **EDUARDO VERÁSTEGUI**—Actor, star of *Bella*

"Abby walked out of the abortion industry and into my office just next door. After seeing her transformation from running a Planned Parenthood clinic to joining our efforts to help women and save lives, I believe that *anyone* can change their mind on abortion." **SHAWN CARNEY**—Campaign Director, 40 Days for Life

"Bold, decisive, and a real trailblazer at Planned Parenthood . . . Abby Johnson, when confronted with reality, was courageous enough to admit her compassion for others was misdirected. Her journey of finding a new way to help women in crisis is truly inspiring." **BOBBY REYNOSO**—Executive Director, Coalition for Life

"Once I began reading this compelling chronicle of compassion, I could not put it down! Abby's narrative points to Christ's story of redemption and will inspire readers for generations to come. *Unplanned* shows that God has a plan and purpose not only for Abby Johnson, but also for you and me, because every life matters."
BRIAN BOONE—President/CEO, Life Centers

"In *Unplanned*, Abby shares intimate details of the happenings that ultimately led her to leave her career as a Planned Parenthood abortion clinic director for 'the other side of the fence,' where she now ardently advocates for the rights of the unborn. If you have ever peacefully protested and prayed for an end to abortion, Abby's story will provide tremendous insights—and encourage you never to give up."
TONY PERKINS—President, Family Research Council

"Abby's story will unsettle your pro-life/pro-choice 'applecart' in a refreshing way. As an abortion-rights advocate, Abby didn't expect to encounter the prayerful, loving, and nonjudgmental outreach to her by pro-lifers. Likewise, pro-lifers who read this book may not expect to meet a Planned Parenthood director who really wanted to reduce abortion. *Unplanned* is a must-read, especially for those of us in the pregnancy center movement—it's reignited our hearts to continue our ministry of compassion to those considering abortion and to always trust in the power of prayer."
MELINDA DELAHOYDE—President, Care Net

"I could not put this book down. Abby's honest and riveting account sheds light on the fact that some Christians are conflicted but satisfied with the goal of 'making abortion safe and rare.' Abby finally had the courage to face the truth about abortion because of the way Christ's love was reflected through the prayer, courage, and support of individual Christians." **MARGARET H. HARTSHORN, PH.D.**—President, Heartbeat International

"'Unplanned' perfectly describes Abby's book from the very first word to the last. Once I started reading, I couldn't put the book down. Abby's story is a must-read for everyone."
BRADLEY MATTES—Executive Director, Life Issues Institute; Host, *Facing Life Head-On* (TV) and *Life Issues* (radio)

"Abby Johnson's powerful story of conversion and repentance reveals how urgently a prayerful, compassionate pro-life presence is needed outside America's abortion clinics. When Abby finally realized the horror of abortion, she knew she could turn for help to the pro-lifers praying outside Planned Parenthood and witnessing to the dignity of every human life. Abby's story should inspire us all to redouble our efforts to bring Christ's love to every abortion clinic in the country."
ANN SCHEIDLER—Vice President, Pro-Life Action League

*un*PLANNED

Abby Johnson

WITH CINDY LAMBERT

The dramatic true story of a former Planned Parenthood *leader's eye-opening journey across the life line*

AN IMPRINT OF
TYNDALE HOUSE PUBLISHERS, INC.

Visit Tyndale online at www.tyndale.com.

Visit Focus on the Family at www.FocusOnTheFamily.com.

TYNDALE is a registered trademark of Tyndale House Publishers, Inc.

Tyndale Momentum and the Tyndale Momentum logo are trademarks of Tyndale House Publishers, Inc. Tyndale Momentum is an imprint of Tyndale House Publishers, Inc.

Focus on the Family and the accompanying logo and design are federally registered trademarks of Focus on the Family, Colorado Springs, CO 80995.

Unplanned: The Dramatic True Story of a Former Planned Parenthood Leader's Eye-Opening Journey across the Life Line

Designed by Jennifer Ghionzoli

Library of Congress Cataloging-in-Publication Data

Johnson, Abby.
Unplanned : the dramatic true story of a former Planned Parenthood leader's eye-opening journey across the life line / Abby Johnson with Cindy Lambert.
p. cm.
Includes bibliographical references.
ISBN 978-1-4143-3939-9 (hc)
1. Pro-life movement—Texas. 2. Abortion—Moral and ethical aspects—Texas. 3. Johnson, Abby. 4. Planned Parenthood Federation of America. I. Lambert, Cindy. II. Title.
HQ767.5.U5J65 2010
363.46092—dc22
[B]
2010043109

ISBN 978-1-4143-3940-5 (sc)

Printed in the United States of America

17 16 15 14 13
8 7 6 5

To my parents,
who have always stood by me and supported me,
no matter what crazy ideas I have fallen for.
There are no better parents in the world.

To my husband and daughter,
whom I always hope to make proud.
I am so thankful that we are on this journey together.
I love you both more than sunshine.

CONTENTS

A Note from Abby Johnson

My story is not a comfortable one to read. I think it's only fair to warn you of that up front. Not comfortable, but honest and true. As you are about to discover, I've spent years on the front lines of the face-off between pro-choice and pro-life advocates. Which side? Both sides. You are about to enter my journey from naive college girl to director of a Planned Parenthood clinic to advocate for families in crisis, including the unborn members of those families.

I reveal my story not because I am proud of it. I am not. But my thinking and choices are not unlike those of so many people I have encountered. And until we each set aside our own preferences for how we *wish* others would think and behave, or how we *assume* others think and behave, we won't be able to understand those with whom we differ in order to engage in real dialogue and discover truth.

I've done my best to be true to my thinking and reasoning *within* each of these stages of my journey—no matter how faulty, how embarrassing, or how politically incorrect—so I suppose that at times you will ask the same questions I've been asked time and again. *Were you really so gullible? Were you really so inconsistent between your values and your actions? Were you really so ambivalent, so naive, so foolish, so . . .* you get the picture. My answer: *Yes.* I've also been asked, *Were you and your pro-choice coworkers really driven by compassion and tenderness, by motives of truly helping women and making the world a better place?* Again, yes.

I often find that people don't like my answers.

That is understandable. My story is not neat and tidy, and it doesn't come wrapped in easy answers. Oh, how we love to vilify our opponents—from both sides. How easy to assume that those on "our" side are right and wise and good; how those on "their" side are treacherous and foolish and deceptive. I have found right and good and wisdom on both sides. I have found foolishness and treachery and deception on both sides as well. I have experienced how good intentions can be warped into poor choices no matter what the side.

To this day I have friends on both sides of this polarizing debate. We all long for a story that shows that "our" side is right and good, and "their" side is wrong and bad, don't we? But I testify that there is good and right and wrong on *both* sides of the fence. And even more shocking—we have far more in common with the "other" side than we might imagine.

But don't slam this book shut because of what I've just said. Read it for that very reason. Read it to understand the surprising hopes and motivations on the "other" side. I was loved from one side onto the other. My hope is that many more thousands will be loved into truth as well. Maybe you will be the one loving someone on the other side of the fence.

So what side of the fence are you on? In all likelihood, as you look through the fence, you see faulty thinking and harmful behavior on the other side. Here's my question for you: are you ready to look through the fence and see goodness, compassion, generosity, and self-sacrifice on the other side?

Did you just feel yourself squirm? If so, welcome to my journey.

Special Note

The names and distinguishing details of some people in this book have been changed, including all Planned Parenthood volunteers and staff. While describing the events in this book, I relied not only on my memory, but on my personal correspondence and interviews with others involved.

CHAPTER ONE

The Ultrasound

CHERYL POKED HER HEAD INTO MY OFFICE. "Abby, they need an extra person back in the exam room. Are you free?"

I looked up from my paperwork, surprised. "Sure."

Though I'd been with Planned Parenthood for eight years, I had never been called into the exam room to help the medical team during an abortion, and I had no idea why I was needed now. Nurse-practitioners were the ones who assisted in abortions, not the other clinic staff. As director of this clinic in Bryan, Texas, I was able to fill in for any position in a pinch, except, of course, for doctors or nurses performing medical procedures. I had, on a few occasions, agreed at a patient's request to stay with her and even hold her hand during the procedure, but only when I'd been the counselor who'd worked with her during intake and counseling. That was not the case today. So why did they need me?

Today's visiting abortionist had been here at the Bryan clinic only two or three times before. He had a private abortion practice about 100 miles away. When I'd talked with him about the job several weeks before, he had explained that at his own facility he did only ultrasound-guided abortions—the abortion procedure with the least risk of complications for the woman. Because this method allows the doctor to see exactly what is going on inside the uterus, there is less chance of perforating the uterine wall, one of the risks of abortion. I respected that about him. The more that could be done to keep women safe and healthy, the better, as far as I was concerned. However, I'd explained to him that this practice wasn't the protocol at our clinic. He understood and said he'd follow our typical procedures, though we agreed he'd be free to use ultrasound if he felt a particular situation warranted it.

To my knowledge, we'd never done ultrasound-guided abortions at our facility. We did abortions only every other Saturday, and the assigned goal from our Planned Parenthood affiliate was to perform twenty-five to thirty-five procedures on those days. We liked to wrap them up by around 2:00 p.m. Our typical procedure took about ten minutes, but an ultrasound added about five minutes, and when you're trying to schedule up to thirty-five abortions in a day, those extra minutes add up.

I felt a moment's reluctance outside the exam room. I never liked entering this room during an abortion procedure—never welcomed what happened behind this door. But since we all had to be ready at any time to pitch in and get the job done, I pushed the door open and stepped in.

The patient was already sedated, still conscious but groggy, the doctor's brilliant light beaming down on her. She was in position, the instruments were laid out neatly on the tray next to the doctor, and the nurse-practitioner was positioning the ultrasound machine next to the operating table.

"I'm going to perform an ultrasound-guided abortion on this patient. I need you to hold the ultrasound probe," the doctor explained.

As I took the ultrasound probe in hand and adjusted the settings on the machine, I argued with myself, *I don't want to be here. I don't want to take part in an abortion.* No, wrong attitude—I needed to psych myself up for this task. I took a deep breath and tried to tune in to the music from the radio playing softly in the background. *It's a good learning experience—I've never seen an ultrasound-guided abortion before,* I told myself. *Maybe this will help me when I counsel women. I'll learn firsthand about this safer procedure. Besides, it will be over in just a few minutes.*

I could not have imagined how the next ten minutes would shake the foundation of my values and change the course of my life.

I had occasionally performed diagnostic ultrasounds for clients before. It was one of the services we offered to confirm pregnancies and estimate how far along they were. The familiarity of preparing for an ultrasound soothed my uneasiness at being in this room. I applied the lubricant to the patient's belly, then maneuvered the ultrasound probe until her uterus was displayed on the screen and adjusted the probe's position to capture the image of the fetus.

I was expecting to see what I had seen in past ultrasounds. Usually, depending on how far along the pregnancy was and how the fetus was turned, I'd first see a leg, or the head, or some partial image of the torso, and would need to maneuver a bit to get the best possible image. But this time, the image was complete. I could see the entire, perfect profile of a baby.

Just like Grace at twelve weeks, I thought, surprised, remembering my very first peek at my daughter, three years before, snuggled securely inside my womb. The image now before me looked the same, only clearer, sharper. The detail startled me. I could clearly see the profile of the head, both arms, legs, and even tiny fingers and toes. Perfect.

And just that quickly, the flutter of the warm memory of Grace was replaced with a surge of anxiety. *What am I about to see?* My stomach tightened. *I don't want to watch what is about to happen.*

I suppose that sounds odd coming from a professional who'd been running a Planned Parenthood clinic for two years, counseling women in crisis, scheduling abortions, reviewing the clinic's monthly budget reports, hiring and training staff. But odd or not, the simple fact is, I had never been interested in promoting abortion. I'd come to Planned Parenthood eight years before, believing that its purpose was primarily to prevent unwanted pregnancies, thereby reducing the number of abortions. That had certainly been *my* goal. And I believed that Planned Parenthood saved lives—the lives of women who, without the services provided by this organization, might resort to some back-alley butcher. All of this sped through my mind as I carefully held the probe in place.

"Thirteen weeks," I heard the nurse say after taking measurements to determine the fetus's age.

"Okay," the doctor said, looking at me, "just hold the probe in place during the procedure so I can see what I'm doing."

The cool air of the exam room left me feeling chilled. My eyes still glued to the image of this perfectly formed baby, I watched as a new image entered the video screen. The cannula—a straw-shaped instrument attached to the end of the suction tube—had been inserted into the uterus and was nearing the baby's side. It looked like an invader on the screen, out of place. Wrong. It just looked wrong.

My heart sped up. Time slowed. I didn't want to look, but I didn't want to stop looking either. I couldn't *not* watch. I was horrified, but fascinated at the same time, like a gawker slowing as he drives past some horrific automobile wreck—not wanting to see a mangled body, but looking all the same.

My eyes flew to the patient's face; tears flowed from the corners of her eyes. I could see she was in pain. The nurse dabbed the woman's face with a tissue.

"Just breathe," the nurse gently coached her. "Breathe."

"It's almost over," I whispered. I wanted to stay focused on her, but my eyes shot back to the image on the screen.

At first, the baby didn't seem aware of the cannula. It gently probed the baby's side, and for a quick second I felt relief. *Of course,* I thought. *The fetus doesn't feel pain.* I had reassured countless women of this as I'd been taught by Planned Parenthood. *The fetal tissue feels nothing as it is removed. Get a grip, Abby. This is a simple, quick medical procedure.* My head was working hard to control my responses, but I couldn't shake an inner disquiet that was quickly mounting to horror as I watched the screen.

The next movement was the sudden jerk of a tiny foot as the baby started kicking, as if trying to move away from the probing invader. As the cannula pressed in, the baby began struggling to turn and twist away. It seemed clear to me that the fetus could feel the cannula and did not like the feeling. And then the doctor's voice broke through, startling me.

"Beam me up, Scotty," he said lightheartedly to the nurse. He was telling her to turn on the suction—in an abortion the suction isn't turned on until the doctor feels he has the cannula in exactly the right place.

I had a sudden urge to yell, "Stop!" To shake the woman and

say, "Look at what is happening to your baby! Wake up! Hurry! Stop them!"

But even as I thought those words, I looked at my own hand holding the probe. I was one of "them" performing this act. My eyes shot back to the screen again. The cannula was already being rotated by the doctor, and now I could see the tiny body violently twisting with it. For the briefest moment it looked as if the baby were being wrung like a dishcloth, twirled and squeezed. And then the little body crumpled and began disappearing into the cannula before my eyes. The last thing I saw was the tiny, perfectly formed backbone sucked into the tube, and then everything was gone. And the uterus was empty. Totally empty.

I was frozen in disbelief. Without realizing it, I let go of the probe. It slipped off the patient's tummy and slid onto her leg. I could feel my heart pounding—pounding so hard my neck throbbed. I tried to get a deep breath but couldn't seem to breathe in or out. I still stared at the screen, even though it was black now because I'd lost the image. But nothing was registering to me. I felt too stunned and shaken to move. I was aware of the doctor and nurse casually chatting as they worked, but it sounded distant, like vague background noise, hard to hear over the pounding of my own blood in my ears.

The image of the tiny body, mangled and sucked away, was replaying in my mind, and with it the image of Grace's first ultrasound—how she'd been about the same size. And I could hear in my memory one of the many arguments I'd had with my husband, Doug, about abortion.

"When you were pregnant with Grace, it wasn't a fetus; it was a baby," Doug had said. And now it hit me like a lightning bolt: *He was right! What was in this woman's womb just a moment ago was alive. It wasn't just tissue, just cells. That was a human baby—fighting for life!*

A battle that was lost in the blink of an eye. What I have told people for years, what I've believed and taught and defended, is a lie.

Suddenly I felt the eyes of the doctor and nurse on me. It shook me out of my thoughts. I noticed the probe lying on the woman's leg and fumbled to get it back into place. But my hands were shaking now.

"Abby, are you okay?" the doctor asked. The nurse's eyes searched my face with concern.

"Yeah, I'm okay." I still didn't have the probe correctly positioned, and now I was worried because the doctor couldn't see inside the uterus. My right hand held the probe, and my left hand rested gingerly on the woman's warm belly. I glanced at her face—more tears and a grimace of pain. I moved the probe until I'd recaptured the image of her now-empty uterus. My eyes traveled back to my hands. I looked at them as if they weren't even my own.

How much damage have these hands done over the past eight years? How many lives have been taken because of them? Not just because of my hands, but because of my words. What if I'd known the truth, and what if I'd told all those women?

What if?

I had believed a lie! I had blindly promoted the "company line" for so long. Why? Why hadn't I searched out the truth for myself? Why had I closed my ears to the arguments I'd heard? Oh, dear God, what had I done?

My hand was still on the patient's belly, and I had the sense that I had just taken something away from her with that hand. I'd robbed her. And my hand started to *hurt*—I felt an actual physical pain. And right there, standing beside the table, my hand on the weeping woman's belly, this thought came from deep within me:

Never again! Never again.

I went into autopilot. As the nurse cleaned up the woman, I put away the ultrasound machine, then gently roused the patient, who was limp and groggy. I helped her sit up, coaxed her into a wheelchair, and took her to the recovery room. I tucked a light blanket around her. Like so many patients I'd seen before, she continued to cry, in obvious emotional and physical pain. I did my best to make her more comfortable.

Ten minutes, maybe fifteen at most, had passed since Cheryl had asked me to go help in the exam room. And in those few minutes, everything had changed. Drastically. The image of that tiny baby twisting and struggling kept replaying in my mind. And the patient. I felt so guilty. I'd taken something precious from her, and she didn't even know it.

How had it come to this? How had I let this happen? I had invested myself, my heart, my career in Planned Parenthood because I cared about women in crisis. And now I faced a crisis of my own.

Looking back now on that late September day of 2009, I realize how wise God is for not revealing our future to us. Had I known then the firestorm I was about to endure, I might not have had the courage to move forward. As it was, since I didn't know, I wasn't yet looking for courage. I was, however, looking to understand how I found myself in this place—living a lie, spreading a lie, and hurting the very women I so wanted to help.

And I desperately needed to know what to do next.

This is my story.

CHAPTER TWO

The Volunteer Fair

I STEPPED INTO MY JUNIOR YEAR at Texas A&M the way most college kids do, I suppose. Knowing I'd made it past the halfway point toward my degree, I shifted my focus toward how and where I would make my mark on the world.

As freshmen, we head into college with high hopes, big dreams, and no small amount of naiveté. At least I had. We plan our majors, take classes, build skills, and worry about assignments, tests, and how to fit in among the thousands of students who seem to already belong in the university world. We approach the world with wide-eyed wonder, open to new directions and eager to make a difference.

By the time our junior year rolls around, we feel like experts at college life, but the big question looming before us grows bigger by the day: *How will I ever make the leap from school to career?*

So it's no surprise that college campuses are the ideal recruiting grounds for all kinds of organizations, especially nonprofits looking for volunteers. Texas A&M was no exception. Every semester there was a volunteer opportunities fair at the student center.

Funny. Seems like with the Big Question hanging over my head, I'd have paid attention to the posters about the upcoming fall volunteer fair. But I hadn't. The only thing on my mind that warm September afternoon in 2001 was that I was hungry and wanted to grab lunch and relax before my next class, so I headed toward the cafeteria through the student center Flag Room. I never dreamed I was about to discover a cause that would ignite my passion and pave the way to a career I would love for nearly a decade.

I admit, when I think back to this day, that I find myself wishing I could speak some wisdom to the gullible, impressionable girl I was. But we can't undo the past, and as mystifying as it is to me now, I clearly see the good intentions that lured me into the organization I would one day flee, and I can still hear the truth woven into the deceptions. And not just the deception I was about to encounter in the Flag Room—also the self-deception that I'd been living, the secret I'd been hiding.

How is it that I made the wrong choices for what seemed to be all the right reasons?

This is the question I am forced to examine on *this* side of the fateful ultrasound-guided abortion. Why did it take me so long—a full eight years—before I could see that, good reasons or not, I'd made the wrong choices? Until I can articulate that answer, how will I grow wise enough to learn from my mistakes? And how can I possibly offer any light to others, whether they're in the pro-life or the pro-choice camp, or are in crisis looking for help? Many of the friends and colleagues working alongside me in the clinic over those years were there for the same reasons—good and noble reasons—that I was. Right reasons, wrong choices.

Since the volunteer fair was held twice every year, the scene of display tables, volunteers, signage, and crowds was no big surprise. The Flag Room at the student center, nicknamed by some the "living room" of A&M, is pretty much the heart of the Aggieland campus, always speckled maroon thanks to the masses of spirit wear–clad students gathering, lingering, eating, laughing, studying, or dozing among the easy chairs, couches, and tables. I always loved the energy of the place—that feeling of being part of history and tradition at Texas's first public institution of higher learning, dating back to 1876. This day, thanks to the fair, the usual hum of hundreds of conversations, accompanied by the ever-present playing of the grand piano in the corner, was magnified to the point of raucous noise. Electricity was in the air. I liked it.

I was in no rush, so I readjusted my sling backpack filled with books and took my time weaving my way through the maze of displays. The nonprofit organizations had tables strewn throughout the room, most manned with recruiters. I was wandering from table to table, picking up pamphlets and reading a few signs, when a table decorated in hot pink caught my attention. It was covered with lots of giveaways—pens, pencils, highlighters, rulers, fingernail files, and hot-pink water bottles. The woman at the table looked friendly and approachable, but still professional and kind of classy. She was fiftyish and slender with stylish blonde hair. I stepped closer and eyed her assortment of pamphlets about services offered by Planned Parenthood.

"Howdy. Are you familiar with Planned Parenthood?" she asked.

I smiled at her use of *howdy*. Here at Texas A&M we considered it our signature welcome. It sounded natural coming from her, so I figured she was a small-town Texan like me.

"Not really. I mean, I've heard of it, but that's about all. So what is it? What do you do?"

"We believe that every community really needs a clinic women can turn to when they find themselves in trouble or needing help. We help women who are facing a crisis."

I liked the sound of that. I was like a magnet for people in crisis. Doug, a friend of mine, always teased me about it. "Abby," he'd say, "you collect strays like some people collect stamps." Strays. His word for people needing a shoulder to cry on, a word of encouragement, a lift to get back in the saddle. But he always smiled when he said it. Like he could talk! While I was an undergrad studying to become a counselor, he was working on his degree in special education. That was one of the things that drew us into friendship. We shared a heart for helping people.

"So what kinds of volunteers are you looking for? What would they do?" I asked.

She told me Planned Parenthood had lots of opportunities. Some volunteers escorted women from their cars into the clinic; others helped with paperwork and filing at their offices. She said Planned Parenthood wanted volunteers who knew how to make women feel cared for, who were compassionate and good with people.

"Our clinics are *so* important to the safety of women," she added. "They can get free birth control there, and abortions if they need them."

My stomach tightened a bit. "Well, I'm not really sure how I feel about abortion. I mean—my family is pro-life and everything, and I guess I've always been pro-life too." I was hoping she couldn't see through me to the inner discomfort she'd just unleashed.

"Oh, I understand." She nodded in seeming approval. I relaxed a bit. *Whew*—so she wasn't going to launch into a pro-life versus pro-choice debate.

If she had, I wouldn't have been able to hold my own. The truth was, I'd never carefully thought through the issues and arguments on both sides. In fact, I'd made it a point to avoid discussions of abortion. But I knew this: I didn't like the thought of appearing to be pro-abortion, no matter what. I love babies and family, and I wanted to be thought of as someone who was pro-family. I found myself vaguely aware of a flicker of inner conflict threatening to rouse itself, but I managed to push it back down and squelch it.

"Our goal at Planned Parenthood is to make abortion rare. Women need to know their options so they can avoid unwanted pregnancy, don't you think?" She was nodding as if she knew we agreed on this.[1]

I felt my eyebrows lift in surprise. I repeated her words, "Your goal is to make abortions rare? How do you mean?"

She explained that Planned Parenthood was the leader in providing community education about birth control. Just imagine, she said, how many abortions could be avoided with only simple information. Because Planned Parenthood made birth control available to women, thousands and thousands of abortions *weren't required.* But when women really did need an abortion, she said, the organization's clinics were vital to their safety.

"Caring for women in crisis is what we are all about," she said. "As a volunteer, you'd see that firsthand."

I could sense her sincerity. I liked her! I could see how much she cared about women. I liked the sound of such a good cause. She could tell.

She pointed out that Planned Parenthood provided not only birth control but annual exams, testing and treatment for sexually transmitted diseases, breast and cervical exams, and sex education. "We are actually the most trusted provider of reproductive health care for women in southeast Texas," she concluded. I was listening carefully. She knew she had me.

"Women have come so far over the years, haven't we? Can you believe that only eighty years ago, we didn't even have the right to vote? And we've had to fight hard for equal pay for equal work and women's rights. But it's pretty unbelievable that even in this day and age, some people want to tell a woman what she can and can't do to take care of her own body."

I nodded. I agreed with equal rights for women. She was making sense to me.

"You said your volunteers escort women into the clinics," I said. "What do you mean? Why do they need escorts?"

She explained that some pretty aggressive anti-choice protesters came to the clinic to use scare tactics to keep women from getting the help they needed. Sometimes they surrounded the clinics and shouted ugly insults at clients, trying to scare them away and shame them. Volunteer escorts met the women at their cars, treated them with calm kindness and reassurance, and walked them into the clinic.

"Our volunteers make a huge difference to these women, especially since so many of them are already scared and confused."

I remembered a day when I'd felt such fear and confusion myself, but I didn't linger on the thought. Instead, I imagined how scary it would be to walk past an angry crowd alone. I'd never attended any kind of protest—I didn't even *know* anyone who had been in a protest. It sounded threatening and alien.

"Does this really happen often enough to need a volunteer staff?" I asked. "I mean, are there really that many people who protest?"

"Oh yes, I'm afraid so." The protesters wanted to take away a woman's right to have an abortion, she said. If abortion were illegal, what would happen to women in crisis pregnancies? Their only choice would be to turn to places that were dangerous to them. And they would wind up injured, damaged, or even dying.

She looked at me with incredulity. "Can you imagine, in this day and age, healthy women like you dying because they can't get access to a safe, proven, legal medical procedure?"

Well, that's just barbaric, I thought, shocked. *I can't imagine that at all. Women shouldn't have to die when there is a safe medical procedure already available! Who'd want to force that on women? Why would they want us to go backward, to take away the right to medical help? While I've been avoiding the issues of abortion's pros and cons, I've had my head buried in the sand!*

Our eyes met, and we both shook our heads in disbelief at the thought of it. Her compassion really captured me—this woman and I were so alike. We both cared about people. Compassion had always been a driving force in my life, part of my identity. It's what had driven me to major in psychology, and it was the very reason I wanted to become a therapist. I really wanted to help hurting people. I was glad I'd met this woman.

"What's your name?" she asked.

"Abby. I'm a junior, working on a bachelor's in psychology."

She held out her hand and we shared a warm handshake. "I'm Jill, and I work in community services for Planned Parenthood." She was just the kind of professional woman I wanted to be. So poised and well-spoken, but still really friendly and kind of small town. I knew I'd like to work with other women like this. If I volunteered, would I get to work with her?

"It's really great to meet you, Abby," Jill said. "So—that's what we are about, and we need volunteers to help because our budget is extremely limited. Many of our services are either free or below cost for our clients. Tell me a little about yourself."

I told her that I loved talking with people and was always drawn to people in crisis. She laughed with me as I told her of Doug's chiding me for my strays. She nodded understandingly as I spelled out my plans to earn a master's in psychology and become a therapist. When I said I was from Rockdale, a small town in Texas, I found out that I'd been right—she was a down-home Texas girl like me. She asked about my family, so I talked about my mom and dad, and how close we were, and my brother who was nine years older than me, whom I didn't get to see too often. She was easy to talk to, and I felt like I had a new friend.

"Abby, you know what I admire about you? You really know where you're headed." I'd be surprised at the number of women who didn't have a clue, she told me. Many women who came to Planned Parenthood's clinics didn't even know their options on how to prevent pregnancy. Or they couldn't afford birth control. Planned Parenthood provided sexual education and free or low-cost birth control, not just to young single girls, but to married women, especially from low-income areas, who couldn't make ends meet as it was.

Because Planned Parenthood was there, she told me, because they listened without judging, shaming, or condemning, women came to their clinics when they needed help. Where else could they go for that?

"It's heartbreaking," she said, shaking her head, "how a few angry protesters can inflict so much shame on these women. And not just over abortion—even over birth control."

"What do you mean?" I was confused. Who would protest

against birth control? I'd never heard of such a thing. I was totally unprepared for Jill's next revelation.

"Here's the sad truth, Abby. The same people who want to stop abortions don't believe in birth control." She told me the pro-lifers not only had no interest in preventing pregnancies, they also wanted to outlaw abortions, forcing women to choose between greater poverty with unwanted babies they couldn't care for or dangerous back-alley butchers.

I imagine I was standing there with my mouth hanging open, trying to figure out why anybody would want that—would want to deny birth control to women, then force them to go somewhere unsafe for an abortion just because they couldn't afford to have another baby. It made no sense. These people claimed to be *against* abortion—so how could they also be against the things that prevent pregnancy and against a woman's right to medical help?

How had I been so unaware of this? How had I come this far in life and not realized what was going on?

This is where I am planting my feet! I decided there on the spot. *I'm getting involved in this. I can help prevent pregnancies, make abortion rare, and make a difference in the lives of women who need help. This is good for women, good for the community, and perfect for me.*

"I'd like to volunteer," I announced. "How do I sign up?"

I filled out the volunteer form, excited that by signing my name I was joining a cause I believed in.

I couldn't wait to get started.

When I look back today on that scene in the Flag Room, my heart breaks. There I was, so young, naive, and unaware. I confess, I am still mystified at how little I knew—not only about the issues of when life begins, but about myself and my ability to make choices that seemed contrary to what I valued.

I'd been part of a small community and a close and loving conservative family. Growing up, I'd attended church weekly, loved God, and cared deeply about my friends and community. I'd been taught that sexual intimacy was for marriage, and I had embraced that as a value. But my behavior hadn't followed my values, and I knew it. Premarital sex, birth control, abortion—other people argued about them. I simply avoided thinking about these issues, about whether they were right or wrong. And somehow, any tensions between what I had been raised to believe and value and what I actually did, I managed to keep hidden in a box buried deep within me. A box I had so far managed to never open, never examine.

I stepped out of the Flag Room that day without any doubt that I'd found a cause—a good cause—to fight for. I would invest myself in serving women in crisis.

How, I wonder still, could I not have recognized the crisis in my own soul?

CHAPTER THREE

The Power of a Secret

Never trust a decision you don't want your mother to know about. How's that for a brilliant insight? These days I can laugh at how obviously true that's been in my life. But the road that finally led me to this wisdom is paved with regret, pain, brokenness, shame, and even blood on my hands.

But I never saw it coming. There was much I didn't see.

I left campus the day of the volunteer fair as a proud champion of women in crisis, their protector against would-be controllers who wanted to rob them of the right to safe medical services and deny them access to education on how to manage their reproductive decisions. I would be their guardian against back-alley butchers; sexually transmitted diseases; unknown cancers lurking in their bodies, undetected for lack of annual exams; and insult-throwing agitators who wanted to humiliate and shame them.

So why didn't I call Mom and tell her my good news?

Mom and Dad lived in Rockdale, about forty-five minutes from

Texas A&M. For the most part, I'd had a great relationship with them and considered myself lucky to have such a close family. Until I left for college, we had always attended church together. I'd been active in church youth group, had been a camp counselor, and always had been a good student—an overachiever in many ways. I'd been vice president of student council, a yearbook editor, active in choir and drama, on the dance team, a member of Business Professionals of America and the Texas Association of Future Educators, and in the top 10 percent of my class. I loved being involved with people and was particularly drawn to leadership opportunities. My parents had always told me they were proud of me and were supportive of me in every way.

At A&M, I called home almost every day just to stay in touch and fill them in on my comings and goings—newsy chats about life, school, and friends. I did the same the day after the fair. I just didn't happen to mention my new decision to become a Planned Parenthood volunteer. It's not that I intended to keep it secret, I told myself—more that I didn't want to worry them, because I didn't think they would be able to understand how the work I would be doing wasn't going to *promote* abortion, but *lessen* it. *I'll wait until I've been doing it a little while,* I reasoned, *so I can give them examples of the good I'm doing there, how I'm helping women.*

It wasn't the first secret I'd kept from them.

Oddly, at the time, I didn't consciously connect this new secret with the old one I still kept. That other secret was about a year old, buried deep, so deep I never let it rise to conscious thought. I lived as if it had never happened, as if it were just a long-ago, unimportant medical appointment that had come and gone without a trace or consequence. It wasn't that I had strong emotions of pain that I was trying to bury. It wasn't festering or lurking or weighing on me.

In fact, I had no emotions at all about it. None. Zip. It was simply a fact—private, personal, done, and behind me. Or so I thought.

"I'm not really sure how I feel about abortion," I'd told Jill in the Flag Room. Truer words were never spoken. I didn't have a clue how I *felt* about abortion, and as for what I *thought* about it—well, I simply didn't.

Though I had grown up in a church that believed in the sanctity of human life, my family had never been the type to debate the ins and outs of this stance, its meaning or consequence, around the kitchen table. But we loved God, and God created life, and people shouldn't take life. Besides, sexual intimacy was kept for marriage, and as long as a woman honored that, she'd never find herself needing to consider an abortion, so it wasn't a matter that I had to give much personal thought to. As a young woman living at home, precollege, I assumed I would live out these values. It really seemed that simple.

It wasn't that simple once I was living at college.

I moved from my small town of Rockdale, with its population of about 5,000, to the home of Texas A&M, only about 55 miles away, in what is affectionately called Aggieland, the Bryan/College Station metropolitan area with a population of about 200,000 people.

Like so many other college freshmen, I enjoyed my first year living on campus at Texas A&M as an experiment in trying on a new persona. I went from superachiever good girl to party girl in a matter of months. Naturally, everything suffered—my grades as well as my choices of friends and activities. I was a classic textbook case of good girl run amok. It didn't take my parents or me long to realize I wasn't where I needed to be, so I transferred to a community college in Bryan, Texas, where I got a grip on my grades. That was the good news. The bad news? I fell head over heels for Mark.

Mark was eight years older than I, and our relationship quickly escalated, emotionally and physically. Mark told me he had a little boy, three-year-old Justin, by a previous marriage. But he never saw Justin, who lived in another town with his mother. In my misguided zeal to come to the rescue of this little boy who didn't see his father, I insisted we contact Justin's mother and begin spending time with Justin. Mark went along halfheartedly, and soon I was picking up Justin for visits. Before long, I'd bonded with Justin as if he were my own son. I became friends with his mom and his maternal grandmother. I reveled in his calling me "my other mom," and I eagerly anticipated every visit.

My parents tried to caution me about the dangers they saw in my relationship with Mark, but I wasn't listening. Mark and I soon got engaged, and I planned to return to Texas A&M and pursue my degree as a married woman with a part-time son.

And then I discovered I was pregnant.

I was worried, scared, and confused. I loved Mark, adored Justin, and was anticipating our life together as a family. I was also looking forward to a few more years of school followed by a meaningful career. I did my best to picture that plan with a baby to care for added into the mix, but I couldn't see how I could make it all work. And telling my parents? I couldn't even imagine it. In my anger over what I had perceived as their lack of support for my relationship with Mark, I already felt I'd nearly ruined our parent-daughter relationship. How could I face them? How could I shame them with the news of a pregnancy before marriage?

Mark, on the other hand, had no illusions about working a baby into our plans. His suggested solution was immediate.

Who was this Abby that I see when I revisit these memories?

I shudder now even just writing down what happened when

I told him the news. "Oh, that's no big problem," he announced matter-of-factly. "You can just have an abortion."

"But, Mark—I don't know how I feel about that. I mean, I just *can't* have a baby now. I'd have to give up school. Still—an abortion?"

"It's easy. Really easy. I've had friends who've done it. It's really no big deal. One appointment and the problem is solved, just like that." Mark informed me that he knew of a clinic in Houston. How did he know of it? He'd taken a previous girlfriend there for an abortion. Now he offered to take me.

The year was 2000. I was twenty years old. Looking back, I find it hard to believe that the values I'd been raised with didn't figure more into my decision making. The high school girl I'd been, the church I'd grown up in, and the family I'd come from—I just put them out of my mind. I've learned a lot since then. I've sat with women of all socioeconomic levels, many races and faiths, from young teen girls to middle-aged women, who have found themselves face-to-face with the same questions and choices I wrestled with.

Today's Abby knows what that Abby did not.

But that Abby, the Abby I was then, agreed. In the space of a few days Mark and I made our plans, and I applied for my very first credit card so I could pay the five-hundred-dollar abortion fee. When the card came in the mail, I called the clinic and made the appointment. I never thought about one simple fact: there was already a baby inside of me. It was as if what I had was not a baby but simply a pregnancy—a medical condition that needed treatment to "cure" it. This pregnancy felt like the heaviest burden I'd ever had to carry—my first true crisis. I'd gotten myself into this. Now I was problem solving to get out of it. To my shame, I don't recall any other thought process than that.

I'd never been to Houston before. The morning of the appointment, I headed southwest on Highway 6 and drove the ninety miles to Houston. Mark was the passenger, the navigator, because he'd been there before. At the clinic, Mark came in with me as I signed in, and we both sat for a brief time alongside a number of girls my age. Then Mark headed outdoors. I was instructed, along with the other women, to move into a back room for a group counseling session. We all watched a brief video that explained the procedure. I can't remember anything about that video today, but I do recall that when it ended, the clinician laughed and said, "Oh, don't be worried, girls." She waved away the video as if it were of no consequence. She had a long braid, twined with beads that caught my eye as her head turned, looking us over. "I've had, like, nine abortions. Really, this will be over before you know it. It's no big deal."

Whoa. Nine? I don't ever want to be like that, I thought. I could tell I wasn't the only one who thought so; several of us made eye contact with raised eyebrows and expressions of disbelief.

"We'll call your name when it's time to come back." She disappeared into the hallway.

That was it. Our "counseling" was evidently over. We sat in silence and waited.

I'm fuzzy on what happened next. My next clear memory is of finding myself lying on a table, feet in stirrups, with a painful pressure steadily increasing in my abdomen. I was groaning, and the nurse was gently rubbing my forearm. "It's okay, honey. It's almost over." I opened my eyes and saw a poster of a cat on the ceiling above my head. The cat was hanging from a branch, and there was a slogan written beneath its dangling feet: *Hang in there.*

But then the cat moved, like it was sliding off the ceiling and onto the wall. "There's something wrong with that picture," I tried to say, but my tongue felt heavy and sluggish.

"You're fine, honey. It's just the medicine. Shhh. Relax."

Another round of pain. I could hear myself groaning, but it sounded distant.

I became vaguely aware that the pain had stopped. I was being moved. The next thing I recall is waking up slumped forward, sitting in a hard, straight chair. I looked around me. My chair was one in a long line, filled by the girls who had watched the video with me. Some were staring at the floor, some rocking with their arms wrapped around their bellies. Some were softly crying. Others, like me, sat silently, repeatedly trying to shift their weight to find a comfortable position. I don't recall any eye contact between us.

I'm not sure how long I sat on that uncomfortable chair, longing to lie down, but then someone was helping me stand and get dressed, right there in the line. I was handed a few crackers. "Here, eat these. Then you can go."

I did as I was told, then walked out. Mark was waiting for me outside, nonchalant and casual. He helped me into the car, and we drove back to Bryan in silence. He dropped me off at my apartment.

The act was done. The "problem" gone. The process had been physically painful, but I had no regrets. No sadness. No struggle over whether what I'd done was right or wrong. Just a definite sense of relief: *Whew. That's behind me. I can get on with my life now.*

I slammed that experience into a box, nailed it shut, stashed it on a shelf in a dark corner of my soul, and pretended it wasn't there. Three days later I resumed my normal activities. I told no one, not a single friend or confidante. It was a secret that only Mark and I knew, but we never spoke of it again. Not once. Several months later, we married.

Today, I wonder if one reason I was so quick, so eager to embrace Jill's presentation about Planned Parenthood—which I heard just about twelve months after that abortion—is that it validated my own secret decision to abort. As Jill spoke, I saw myself as one of the wise and lucky ones who had control over my reproductive rights and utilized my access to safe medical procedures. Jill clearly didn't look down on the decision to abort. She understood the crises women found themselves in. In my role at Planned Parenthood, I would be helping other women exercise their "rights" and protect their "access" as they faced their crises.

Had I never had an abortion—had I never personally bought into the thinking that if the "embryonic tissue" inside of me was simply removed, I could get on with my life and not be hindered by my "mistake"—how would I have responded to Jill's well-crafted presentation designed to enlist college girls into the ranks of Planned Parenthood?

I'll never know. That is one of the costs of my well-kept secret.

Once it had taken hold within me, my secret had the power to shape and influence my reasoning, my perspective, my conscience. Years later, I would discover that the box in my soul wasn't sealed as well as I'd thought. It was releasing undetectable yet poisonous fumes that wafted through my soul in silence and contaminated my heart. Over time, this secret did to me the same thing I did in my relationship with the parents who'd given birth to me and nurtured, supported, and loved me with their whole hearts. It hid itself, just as I was now hiding my true self from my parents. The insidious power that my secret wielded in my soul was kept secret *from me.*

Now that my secrets are out, their power is broken, and my vision has cleared enough to see with new eyes the road that led me to this place. It is a road worth revisiting, for here I am discovering for the first time what parts are paved with regret, remorse, or brokenness. But to my surprise there are bright spots along the way as well. I've encountered deep friendship and loyalty, and people of true strength. In the women I met in the Planned Parenthood clinic where I worked in Bryan, Texas—both clients and staff—I've seen courage and resilience. And on both sides of the fence that encircles that clinic, I've found compassion and community. I have also faced death threats and known the murder of a friend. I've been dragged into court, turned away from some churches, welcomed by others. I've discovered that perceived enemies were friends, and I've had perceived friends declare me an enemy.

Above all, I've discovered that the road that led me here is being resurfaced now, with grace. I've been given new eyes—eyes now able to see grace doing its work.

This road runs straight from the Texas A&M Flag Room to 4112 East 29th Street in Bryan, Texas. I've driven the short three miles many times. To pull into the driveway of that particular Planned Parenthood clinic, you have to pass through a black iron gate in the six-foot-tall iron fence that encircles the clinic. I clearly remember my first time passing through that gate as a volunteer.

To revisit my journey, this is where I must go next.

CHAPTER FOUR

The Cause

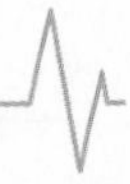

THE FIRST TIME I pulled into the parking lot of the Planned Parenthood clinic in Bryan, Texas, I was a bit creeped out by the six-foot-high iron fence encircling the building and lot. Clearly the fence was designed to keep something locked in, or something locked out. I just wasn't sure which. I didn't have a clue how dramatically my own answer to that question would shift over time, nor did I foresee the powerful role this fence was going to play—and in fact, still plays—in my life.

I'm just here to check this out, I told myself to quiet my nervousness. *If I don't like it, I'm not obligated to come back.* Only one week had passed since I'd signed up at the fair, and I hadn't exactly been trained for what I was about to encounter. All I knew was what Jill told me at the volunteer fair and a few brief instructions given me over the phone in a follow-up call—where to park (on a side street near the clinic), what time to come (about 6:50 a.m.), and how long I'd stay (about two hours).

The Bryan clinic is located on a mostly residential portion of 29th Street in a neighborhood filled, for the most part, with ranch houses built in the 1950s and 1960s. Most of the homes sit on quarter-acre grass lots. No other fences caught my attention that day, so as I approached the clinic, I found the fence terribly out of place.

Before parking, I wanted to check out the building entrance. I pulled through the open gate that spanned a wide cement driveway and turned around in the small lot set between the fence and the building. Looking out my windshield at the iron bars gave me the distinct feeling of being in prison. *Not exactly a welcoming view,* I thought. *I wonder why they need the fence.* I had not yet grasped the sense of "war" between the pro-choice and pro-life causes in Bryan. My education was about to begin.

I was surprised how small and unassuming the building was. Built of light-gray brick, the ranch-style office was not much different in shape and size from the homes surrounding it, though the short, wide driveway leading into the small parking lot, the line of windows facing the lot, and the glass entry door definitely had the look of an office rather than a home.

I'd arrived early—about 6:40 a.m. My shift was 7:00 to 9:00 a.m., but I wanted time to get acclimated before I was on duty. I really had no idea what to expect, even though the recruiter, Jill, had told me in general terms the duties of a volunteer escort. I had worried that morning about what to wear. Do I dress up? Go business casual? Jeans? What will everyone else be wearing? In the end, I dressed up a bit—dress slacks, a nice turquoise short-sleeved shirt, comfortable yet dressy shoes.

But after I'd moved my car to a side street and walked back to the clinic, I noticed the other volunteers, three that morning, were wearing cargo shorts and T-shirts! They said, "What are you wearing? Don't you realize it's going to be burning up out there today?" And besides, they gave me a vest, standard wear for all volunteers so they're instantly identifiable to clients as someone official from the clinic. So who cared what I had on underneath it? No one could see it anyway. Those vests were royal blue back then. Later, we changed them to a bright, highlighter yellow. The rest of the Planned Parenthood staff—clinicians, nurses, office personnel, and the director—all wore scrubs of various colors.

I'd only been there a few minutes before I met Cheryl, the clinic director. Unlike Jill, Cheryl was all business and paired me up with a more experienced escort, who filled me in on my duties.

This volunteer explained that we would wait outside by the front door. When a client pulled up, we were to head to her car immediately so someone was there when she opened her door. By the time the clinic opened, the pro-lifers would be on the other side of the fence, she said. They showed up every Tuesday because they knew it was abortion day. When the client opened her door, we were to start talking right away. We could talk about anything—the weather, her clothes, her car—anything to distract her from the voices through the fence. They'd be harassing her, and we wanted to make sure our voices were the ones she heard.

"You walk with me the first few times to get a feel for it, okay?" she said as she ended her overview of my job.

It was all so strange. By 7:00, pro-lifers had begun to show up outside the fence. It was still fairly cool that first morning, which was good since I was ridiculously overdressed. We stepped outside to start our shift. I was extremely uneasy. As I waited, I was caught off guard by a few protesters on the other side of the fence. One fellow was dressed up as the Grim Reaper—he even carried a scythe. A woman took a spot outside the fence and began waving a huge placard with a picture of an aborted fetus on it—a grotesque image. I couldn't imagine why she'd be so cruel as to show it in public. Every now and then she'd shout out some antiabortion slogan. Not everyone was so dramatic. In fact, some people gathered and just stood silently, and a few prayed in small groups.

The first client pulled her car into the lot, and I shadowed my trainer as she rushed to the opening car door. "How are you today? I hope you didn't have any trouble finding us. Nice weather this morning, huh?" The young woman was half listening to my trainer and half doing what I was doing—peering through the fence to see who these people were.

I could hear a voice from the other side of the fence.

"Hi, I'm here from Coalition for Life. We can help you today if you like. We have alternatives to offer you. You don't have to go through with this today." My trainer did her best to talk over the voice by asking about traffic while pretending there was not another voice competing with her own. I was curious, though, to hear what the voice was saying.

Who are these people? Are they college kids like me? I wondered. *Why are they here so early on a Tuesday morning, and what do they think they are going to accomplish? Do they all know each other? Do they plan this out together?* My trainer kept up her chatter as we led our client away from the fence and through the door. A clinic worker greeted and escorted her to a waiting area, and we returned to the front door. And so it went, a surprisingly steady stream of clients while the same scripts on both sides of the fence were repeated time and again.

Between clients my trainer fed me general information about the women who came to the clinic. A relatively small percentage of the clients who came for an abortion were minors, she told me. The majority of women coming for abortions were in their twenties. Some women in their thirties came as well, though not as many.[2]

I asked whether most clients were single women who were pregnant for the first time. She told me it varied more than I'd think. Some were married, many not; some had kids already at home and maybe too many mouths to feed. Others were pregnant for the first time. Some of the clients were working women; some were just students who were scared and alone. Given the fact that Bryan is mostly white, most clients were white too, but again, that varied, not only because of the college population, but also because there weren't many places in this part of Texas to get an abortion. Lots of women, she said, drove a good distance to get to the clinic.

I thought of my own abortion just a year before and the long drive I'd made to Houston. I hadn't even known about this place then.

"Why do the pro-lifers assume all the women coming in are having abortions?" I asked her. "Planned Parenthood offers all kinds of services, right? Pap smears and pregnancy testing and ultrasounds, right?"

"Yeah, but not on abortion days. On Tuesdays we mostly do just abortions, and they know that. Okay," she said as another car pulled into the lot. "Your turn this time. I'll walk with you, but you do the talking. Are you ready?"

I was there the moment the new client opened her car door.

"Hi. I'm glad you found us okay. I'll walk you to the door."

"We know this is a hard day for you," another voice chirped during my brief pause. "We are out here because we care about you." My immediate thought was that if they cared about this woman, they wouldn't look so frightening with a Grim Reaper and a huge photo of an aborted fetus on display. That certainly didn't look caring to me. My client turned her head to see who had spoken through the fence. My eyes followed hers for a second and landed on a young woman about my age.

"Sorry about these people," I spoke up, drawing her attention back to me. "Let's get inside."

Just then someone at the fence shouted, "Abortionists are murderers! Repent!"

"Starting to warm up, isn't it? I love the color of your shirt." I was groping for words but could hear how ridiculous I sounded in light of the accusation we'd just heard. Another voice was talking over me, now calling louder, as the client and I were heading toward the building.

"We have alternatives for you if you don't want to go through with this today," a man's voice called. The client's eyes locked on mine, and I saw anxiety there.

"And here we are. Let me get the door for you," I offered in as soothing a voice as I could, now feeling I needed to protect her. I walked her to the receptionist. "Here we go. She'll help you now."

"Thank you," the girl answered timidly, her eyes on the floor. She looked frightened.

I gently patted her arm, then left her with the receptionist and went back outside, feeling a bit rattled.

The trainer said I'd done a great job talking to the patient while keeping her moving. "We need to do all we can to protect our clients from those pro-lifers," she added. "See that guy over there?" She pointed to a man on the other side of the fence who looked about ten years older than me.

"Yeah. Who is he?"

"That's David Bereit. He's the director of Coalition for Life. Their office is just down the street." She went on to explain that the group's purpose was to turn the community against us and shut us down.

I looked through the fence at the pro-lifers assembled there. Some college-age kids, guys and girls, stood praying together with heads bowed; two young moms with strollers simply stood and looked on; a middle-aged couple walked the fence, speaking to another client being escorted toward the clinic door. The costumed Grim Reaper just lurked, occasionally waving his scythe in the air. A gray-haired man had shown up and was strolling back and forth carrying a big handmade sign crudely lettered "MURDERERS" in red paint. The woman with the aborted fetus picture was marching back and forth, raising and lowering it like she was on parade. A young couple stood holding a simple sign that read "CHOOSE LIFE."

This is unbelievable, I thought. *What have I stepped into?* It was like a face-off through the fence. A war zone. The tension in the air was palpable.

Another volunteer took the next car, and I just watched. Clients had two parking options when they pulled in. They could turn left to park facing the fence like I originally had, or right to park facing the building. This client parked facing the fence. A friendly looking young woman outside the fence, about my age, stepped forward, pressed herself against the fence, and spoke softly to the client the second she opened her car door. From my spot by the front door I couldn't hear what she said, but the client paused and listened. The woman outside the fence had a kind face and continued speaking in quiet tones. The Planned Parenthood volunteer was trying in vain to get the client's attention but hadn't been fast enough. I watched as the client stepped toward the fence, then she and the pro-lifer walked side by side with the fence between them toward the open gate, where they came face-to-face.

"Uh-oh. They got one," my trainer said. "I wish they'd leave these poor women alone. Do they have to harass them over such a personal decision? Why can't they just accept that not everybody sees the world as black and white as they do?"

I watched as the pro-lifer handed our client some literature—she didn't look like she felt harassed to me. Clearly, she'd chosen to talk to the pro-lifer. Her Planned Parenthood escort stood glaring at the pro-lifer for a moment before managing to get the client's attention. The two then walked into the building.

I felt confused. That client had looked truly interested in the information from the pro-lifer. *If we are pro-choice*, I thought, *then we believe in women making their own choices, right? So why do we feel we need to protect clients from conversations about their choices? What does it hurt if they hear information and make the choice to leave? We want them to consider their alternatives and to make the decision that's right for them. Right?* I found myself wondering if I belonged here.

But another look across the fence jolted me from such thoughts—the marching woman with the horrid photo, the Grim Reaper now waving his scythe silently in the air, the sign with blood-red letters spelling out *MURDERERS*. Some of these people hardly seemed balanced, helpful, or reasonable. Clearly, they had an agenda of their own. *They aren't here offering women choices*, I thought. *They just don't want them to choose abortion*. I thought of the professional demeanor of the clinic director, Cheryl; the sparkling clean office inside with clinicians, a doctor, ultrasound equipment; all of the professionals able to offer cancer screening and STD testing. Surely we were on the right side, weren't we?

Unsettled, I found myself looking forward to the end of my shift.

When my two-hour shift was finally up, I couldn't wait to hand in my vest. I walked briskly toward my car, down the street. The female pro-lifer with the kind face I'd watched earlier fell in beside me.

"Hi. I'm Marilisa. I don't think I've seen you here before," she said.

"No. It's my first day."

I wasn't sure what to expect from her, and I was a bit on guard. She was about my age—in fact, we're only six months apart, we found out later—and she seemed nice.

"Can you tell me why? Why you're volunteering?" she asked.

"Well—I don't know for sure that I'll be coming back. I'm just kind of checking it out."

"May I ask your name?"

"Abby."

She looked more serious then, and she said, "Abby, do you know they perform abortions?"

I'm not sure why I let my guard down so completely with her, a woman I'd never met before who definitely worked on the other side of the fence, but I told her something I'd told almost no one else at that point: "I've had an abortion myself. It was a decision I made, and I don't have a problem with other women making the same decision."

She nodded and looked thoughtful. "I'm so sorry you had to experience that, Abby."

I was a little taken aback by the kindness in her voice.

"No, I'm okay with it, really. It was my decision. No one forced me."

"All right. But you know, Abby—if you ever need help with any of that—"

And just then we heard a shout. It was Cheryl, the clinic director, literally hollering from just outside the side door of the clinic. "Leave her alone, Marilisa!" Her voice pierced the air.

I remember being startled. It had actually been a pretty pleasant conversation up to that point. Marilisa wasn't bothering me; I didn't think she was being aggressive or out of line. In fact, I thought her genuinely kind. I understood now why our client had been drawn to talk with her through the fence.

Then Cheryl hollered again: "Go on and get in your car, Abby."

I said good-bye and did as I was told.

That first day had been an eye-opener, and not a pleasant one. I left the clinic unsure whether I would be coming back. In fact, I didn't go back the following Tuesday, and when I got a call from Planned Parenthood inviting me to return, I said, "No, not this time. Call me next time." But I said the same thing the next time, too. There was a tug-of-war going on inside. Did I really want to do this? It wasn't fun, it wasn't comfortable, and it left me confused. Was I really committed to this cause in the face of how uneasy I'd been?

In the end, I decided that my comfort level didn't matter. The thought I kept coming back to was my conversation with Jill at the volunteer fair, now combined with the creepy Grim Reaper and the red-lettered word *MURDERERS* thrust in the face of scared young women. If abortions weren't legal and available, women in crisis would get them anyway, but they would have to settle for unsafe and unsanitary abortions from someone who in all likelihood wouldn't be adequately trained. Women would die. Planned Parenthood was helping to prevent that.

And if women did decide to exercise their right, they needed a friendly voice to walk them past that wacky crowd. If all the people at the fence had been like Marilisa, escorts wouldn't be needed, I reasoned. But some of the pro-lifers were just plain nuts as far as I was concerned.

I didn't yet understand that the pro-lifers outside the clinic that day weren't a unified, like-minded group; that many didn't even know each other. To me, they looked together, all gathered on "their" side of the fence. So I wrongly assumed everyone was part of the same organization—this Coalition for Life a few of them had mentioned through the fence. And I didn't approve of the mean-spirited approach of frightening, sickening images and accusatory, inflammatory signs. How could this be helpful or appealing to women who were scared and desperate? What were the pro-lifers trying to accomplish with such methods? I was grateful I hadn't encountered such a demonstration on the day I'd gotten an abortion.

In the end I decided, *All right. I'll go. I'll give it another shot.*

Once I'd decided that, my thought processes changed. From that point on, those people on the other side of the fence—the pro-life protesters, the placard wavers, the shouters, the Grim Reaper—became the enemy. My cause—helping women in crisis—was just, I believed, and they were the ones opposing that just cause. So I had to oppose them. With conviction. I wouldn't be rude, I wouldn't shout—I would even try to be friendly to this obviously misguided group. I didn't see any reason to be hostile with them. But I would be definite and direct and firm.

In the years to come, though I didn't have a clue at this point, I would actually come to value some of these pro-lifers as friends. I would witness a careful and hard-won shift in the techniques, tone, and character of the pro-life advocates outside the Planned

Parenthood fence. By my first shift at the fence in September 2001, the Bryan clinic had been providing abortions for about two years, and the pro-life movement of the area was in its infancy. Though I didn't know it then, I'd already met one of the courageous and prayerful leaders who would go on to shape the Coalition for Life: Marilisa. And one of the young college-age guys praying that day, Shawn Carney, would soon marry Marilisa and assume leadership of the organization. Together with David Bereit, they would help transform the efforts here in Bryan into a powerfully positive pro-life force whose influence would reach across the country and to other continents as well. These pioneers would replace the shouting with gentle conversation, the waving of ugly signs with prayerful vigils, and the hostility with a peaceful presence. They would also change my life. But all of that was yet to come.

On my first day as a Planned Parenthood volunteer, the confrontational and hostile demeanor of a few in the pro-life crowd not only colored my perception of their movement but solidified my commitment to Planned Parenthood. Though my first day had been baffling, one thing was clear to me: those on *my* side of the fence were defending and helping women, as we protected them from those on the other side of the fence.

I'd discovered the answer to my question about the fence. Obviously, I thought, it was there to keep those hostile pro-lifers out and provide a safe haven for the women in need of Planned Parenthood's services.

CHAPTER FIVE

The Bond of Compassion

LOBBY DAY IS JUST WHAT IT SOUNDS LIKE.

Every other year Planned Parenthood and other pro-choice groups gather students, staff, and supporters to descend upon the Texas legislature in Austin, Texas's capital. February 2003 marked my initiation into this much-celebrated part of the Texas political process and cemented my identity as a vital part of the Planned Parenthood movement.

For weeks leading up to the event, Planned Parenthood had been publicizing it to clinic staff as well as to students at Texas A&M, and I was psyched! We gathered at the clinic at 6:00 a.m. on a chilly morning and piled into a bus that took us to a meeting hall in Austin where hundreds of others from around the state had gathered. Hot pink, our signature color, was everywhere. We were given hot pink canvas bags and water bottles, and many of us wore hot pink hats, shirts, or scarves. We rallied together, listened to speeches, studied our packets of talking points, and prepared to meet our legislators.

Today, the speakers told us, we were personally taking part in the political process of our great nation, many of us for the very first time. Perhaps before we had exercised our right to vote; today we would lobby by personally conversing with our political representatives. We were told we should be proud to represent Planned Parenthood, the world's largest and most trusted reproductive health care organization. Planned Parenthood believed that everyone had the right to choose when or whether to have a child, that every child should be wanted and loved, and that women should be in charge of their own destinies. Every year, we were reminded, nearly 25,000 affiliate volunteers and staff provided sexual and reproductive health care, education, and information to nearly five million women, men, and teens in the United States. More than two million Planned Parenthood donors and activists also served as advocates for sexual and reproductive rights. "You are a part of this great cause," one speaker announced. My heart swelled with pride.

After the speech-making we were divided into teams and sent to the offices of legislators, some of whom supported us, some of whom opposed our position. We were to voice our support of Planned Parenthood and the pro-choice movement using the talking points we'd been given. We met with officials or their appointed staff. I found myself the spokesperson in several meetings, passionately saying, "The only way to reduce the number of abortions is to reduce the number of unintended pregnancies. The only way to reduce the number of unintended pregnancies is to provide additional funding for contraception."

I firmly believed in our cause, and I'd been well educated by Planned Parenthood to push for our public education system to provide better sex education and hand out contraceptives. I loved being part of this massive wave of pink washing over the capitol.

I'd never felt so proud of my citizenship and so proud of my part in Planned Parenthood. My actions, I believed, were helping to reduce the number of abortions.[3]

By this time I'd been a volunteer at the Bryan clinic for about a year and a half, but as I rode back to Bryan that night in the bus filled with fellow supporters, I knew I'd never before felt such a connection with others. It was a bond that would continue to grow.

And I was at a point in my life when I needed to feel as if I belonged. That same month, I separated from Mark and filed for divorce. He and I had married in December 2001, about a year after my abortion and just a few months after I'd joined Planned Parenthood. I had dropped out of school for a time—partly to increase my working hours to cover living expenses, but also because I'd lost my way at school once Mark and I got involved. Our marriage had been rocky from the start as I'd soon discovered that trust and fidelity weren't part of his plan for marriage, and I had sadly come to realize that my parents' words of caution—though unwelcomed by me—had been well founded.

Though the marriage had been painful, I'd deeply invested myself in my relationship with Mark's son, Justin, now seven years old. I loved this little boy like my own and treasured each visit we had with him. But Mark had recently told me that he had no intention of continuing his visits with Justin and was preparing to sign over his parental rights entirely to Justin's mother. She and I had developed a good relationship as we'd coordinated Justin's trips to visit us, so I knew he'd be in excellent hands, but I was sorely grieving the reality that I'd have to say good-bye to this precious little guy. How could I, his father's soon-to-be ex-wife, merit visitation rights? I knew I didn't, and I knew it wouldn't be fair for me even to ask for them. The grief had been haunting me for weeks.

So as I drove home on the bus that night, I found comfort in feeling a part of something bigger than myself, something I believed was doing so much good in the lives of others.

I'd expanded my volunteer work at the clinic since my early days as a patient escort. Many of the pro-lifers' faces had become familiar to me by then. Marilisa and I often said hello, and Shawn Carney and I would nod or say hi. David Bereit was almost always there as well. Cheryl and some of the other Planned Parenthood staff ignored them all, and they pretty much avoided her, but a few of us frequently exchanged greetings or nods with the friendly ones. I knew these people saw me as an enemy to the cause of life, but I took pride in my work, drawing upon the sense of purpose that came from knowing I was helping women in crisis.

I still escorted on abortion days, which had by then switched to Wednesdays and would eventually change to every other Saturday, but now I also came in nearly every weekend as well, helping out in the office and pitching in anywhere I was needed. I felt valuable and wanted at the clinic.

A few weeks after Lobby Day, however, I hit a crisis of my own. I discovered I was pregnant for a second time. Panic and grief overwhelmed me, as did the feeling of utter failure. I felt I'd failed at sticking to school, failed at my marriage, and now my contraception method had failed as well. My soon-to-be ex-husband was about to sign away his paternal rights to his own seven-year-old son, so I knew he wasn't interested in being a father, and I wasn't at all prepared to consider becoming a self-supporting single mother. Besides, I no longer wanted to be connected to this man, and if I were to have his child, I'd be connected to him for the rest of my life.

Even as I write that sentence I hear the faulty thinking that plagues every woman considering an abortion—thinking expressed in the phrase *if I have this child.*

If I have this child? Why wasn't it obvious to me that I *already had a child,* who was growing inside of me? Once you are pregnant, there is no *if.* That child, though tiny and in an early stage of development, *already exists*! But I didn't yet see that. What I saw, and by now was reinforcing in the minds of other young women as part of the Planned Parenthood organization, was that I was in a *condition of pregnancy*, not that I was now the mother of a child already dependent upon my own body for sustenance. I am amazed at how semantics can shape thought.

I thought of my parents and knew they'd be compassionate and supportive, that they'd help me in every way, but I couldn't bear the thought of the burden this would create for them. At least, that's what I told myself at the time. I can see now that I never gave my parents enough credit—not in my out-of-wedlock first pregnancy with Mark, and not in this second pregnancy coming just as I was about to be divorced. Frankly, looking back, I suspect that by keeping it a secret from my parents, I was trying to avoid it becoming "real" for me. I better understand now that my parents are made of tough stuff and can not only handle whatever life throws at them, but can, through their love and support, help me do the same.

When I'm asked today what someone might have said to get me to change my mind about having either abortion, I tell them it would be this: "What do you think would disappoint your parents most? To find out that you'd gotten pregnant, or to learn that you had taken the life of their grandchild?" Looking back, I realize my fear of talking with my parents about my crisis pregnancies was really irrational.

I so wish I could write that I agonized long and hard over my choices for this pregnancy. But I'd be lying. The truth is that abortion had by now become a simple and normal reality in my life. Every week I walked alongside women on their way to ending their pregnancies and wished them well a few hours later as they headed back out the door. Now, without even revealing my pregnancy to Mark, I made that same appointment for myself.

I know—this chapter fully reveals the ugly truth. I was completely inconsistent in my own thoughts and values. I lobbied at the state capitol for abortion rights while telling myself proudly that, by helping prevent unwanted pregnancies, I was helping reduce the number of abortions. Yet now I was scheduling another abortion myself because I was in a crisis pregnancy.

It's embarrassing to even read my own words here. But it's important that I write them. It's important that you read them. My story—my decision to abort my second pregnancy even though I told myself I was a champion for decreasing the number of abortions—illustrates the complexity, the confusion, and frankly, the disconnect between behavior and values that permeates our culture. I spent many years counseling women whose thought patterns were not unlike my own. Consider this statistic from the Guttmacher Institute, the research arm of Planned Parenthood: nearly two-thirds of women who have abortions identify themselves as Christian.[4] I was one among many.

Unlike the day I went in for my first abortion, I was extremely well-educated this time. At our clinic we always did an ultrasound before an abortion to confirm how far along the pregnancy was, and we offered the patient the choice to view a photo of the fetus. Like most, I declined to view the photo. I was eight weeks along, and that made me eligible for a medication abortion (the cutoff is nine weeks) using RU-486, also known as Mifeprex, the abortion pill. As I'd witnessed women choosing between medication or surgical abortions, it seemed to me that for early abortions, the medication abortion was the more private, less invasive, more comfortable way to go. And it appeared to offer more control. No anesthesia, no surgery—just a few pills, right?

My experience proved otherwise.

As is typical, I took one pill, Mifeprex, while at the clinic. That pill separates the pregnancy from the lining of the uterus so that it is no longer viable. (Did you notice I said "pregnancy"? Again, the power of semantics. Our Planned Parenthood terminology reinforced that we were removing an unwanted pregnancy, not killing a fetus.) I was also given an antibiotic, then sent home with a prescription for a painkiller and an antinausea medication to take as needed, in addition to pills called misoprostol to be taken between twenty-four and forty-eight hours later, which would complete the process of cleaning out the uterus.

The days that followed, alone in my apartment, were sheer agony. If all had worked as it should have, I would have passed the fetus within the first six to eight hours and the rest of the uterine lining within about forty-eight hours. But nothing went as "advertised." Of course, since the law requires "informed consent," I had been told about possible complications such as severe cramping, hemorrhage, and infection. And I had been instructed to call and to return to the clinic if I suffered these side effects. I'd also been instructed to return for a follow-up visit. I was, however, a very bad patient.

My cramping was excruciating and went on for days and days. I was too ill to get out of bed, ran a fever, and bled heavily. I was frightened, but whether out of shame, humiliation, or self-punishment—

or maybe some combination of the three—I would not call the clinic. I couldn't bear the thought of going to an emergency room or an ob-gyn because there was no way I was going to confess that I'd brought this on myself by aborting my second pregnancy. My phone kept ringing and ringing as the clinic tried to reach me for follow up, but I wouldn't answer. I mentioned nothing to my parents by phone. I suffered alone.

After two weeks I returned to work though I still felt so weak I'd come home exhausted and go straight back to bed. Finally, after about eight weeks of feeling ill, I felt recovered enough to return to the clinic for one of my volunteer shifts.

"Abby, where have you been? What happened to you? Are you okay? We've been worried sick about you! Why wouldn't you answer?"

"Oh, I'm sorry. I'm fine. Just so busy with work and everything. Sorry I worried you." And that's all I told them.

In the months that followed, I tried to just put the entire event out of my mind. I said my final tearful farewell to Justin, and my divorce from Mark was finalized in December 2003. I don't think I was ever more relieved to bid farewell to a year. But as I did, I recognized two bright spots in what had otherwise been a year of heartbreak.

The first was Lobby Day, which had galvanized my commitment to Planned Parenthood. The second was my decision to throw myself back into school and complete my psychology major at Texas A&M. In the aftermath of my grief-filled spring, I'd determined to move forward and overcome my failures. I knew I wanted to give to others, perhaps as a counselor or therapist, or maybe through the Peace Corps or teaching. Whatever I chose, I decided, I was going to be a leader and would fight for those who needed advocates. In contrast to my earlier college years, now that I had a sense of direction, I threw myself into my studies with a passion, and my grades showed it.

By spring of 2004, my increased volunteer role at Planned Parenthood took a new turn: I became the campus intern at Texas A&M. Given my heavy school schedule, it was ideal, since I was spending all my time on campus anyway. The role took approximately ten hours a week, though it varied a good bit. Whenever the school held a health fair, I'd set up a table to equip students with health information. I talked to students about STD and HIV screening as well as contraception alternatives. I loved my new Planned Parenthood role, and it seemed to fit perfectly with my desire to counsel and teach.

With Planned Parenthood now playing a greater part in my life, I decided to tell my parents about my volunteer work for the organization. My method of easing into the topic is a good indicator of a game I was playing with myself. When I mentioned it the first few times, I emphasized that I was working at a Planned Parenthood health clinic for women. I suspect my parents weren't really aware at the time of what Planned Parenthood was all about. Fortunately, my mom didn't ask if they did abortions, and I certainly didn't bring it up. Over time, though, the subject worked its way into our conversations, and when it did, I was sure to emphasize the talking points I'd learned for Lobby Day.

"You know, Mom, Planned Parenthood's goal is to make abortion rare, so we really emphasize ways to prevent unwanted pregnancy."

One day I had a conversation with a longtime friend who, when I told her of my work with Planned Parenthood, got quite upset with me. The next day I complained about this to my mom over the phone. It became crystal clear to me that Mom also disapproved of the organization where I worked.

"Well, Abby, you work at an abortion clinic. People don't like that. It's one of the most controversial places in the country to work. If this is what you plan to do, you'd better get used to the fact that lots of people are not going to approve. If that's something you can't handle, then you need to find some other place to work."

You've gotta love my mom—she tells it like it is. I chalked her reaction up to old-fashioned thinking. But to her credit she didn't let it become a barrier in our relationship. She and my dad still welcomed my daily calls, loved me, and kept the bond between us strong. In that they never wavered.

That spring brought another development to my life. In March, my friend Doug (yes, the same one who teased me about collecting strays) and I began dating. Doug and I shared many of the same passions—teaching, making the world a better place, caring for people facing difficulties. Doug was at nearby Sam Houston State University studying to become a special education teacher. He was kind and compassionate and had a great sense of humor. He was also a Christian whose faith was an important part of his life. I was drawn to him for all those reasons, but I particularly admired how his faith shaped his values and choices. I sensed a strength and consistency in his life—an integration of his beliefs with his practices—which I knew was lacking in my own life. Even more, I felt he accepted and cared about me without judging me, and that acceptance made me feel safe enough to share my story with him, including the truth about both my abortions.

Doug didn't approve of abortion, yet he didn't punish me. Instead he engaged me in lively discussions that challenged my reason and logic—or perhaps I should say my lack of them. I confess, I am never one to back away from a good debate, so when we'd get into such discussions I'd come out swinging.

"Doug, the real issue is viability. I don't approve of late-term abortions at all, because by that time the fetus has become viable and could live outside the womb. But before that, it's just an undeveloped fetus that couldn't possibly survive on its own. If it is an unwanted pregnancy, isn't it better to offer the woman a safe alternative to end it early on?"

"Abby, how can you think that? You're a smart person. We're talking about a baby from the start, at two weeks or six, at twelve weeks or twenty. How can it be okay to abort at eight weeks but not at sixteen? Viability shifts as medical science improves. Are you saying that the measure of what is human, what is moral or immoral, flexes as science advances?"

And we'd go on. I'd dig in, he'd question back, but it didn't escalate to contempt. Instead, we each felt cared for and respected by the other. Doug admired my heart for the clients. I'd tell him about the situations of the women who came in, not just those seeking abortions, but women dealing with all sorts of issues—abuse, rape, poverty, illness. I'd tell him the ways we helped those women, and I could tell that he cared too.

I'd also tell him about the pro-lifers. I knew he'd enjoy hearing about one of the regulars at the fence. I poked fun at some of the more outlandish antics and griped about those who caused a scene. But I also kept him up to speed on some of the regulars.

"Doug, have I told you about Mr. Orozco?"

"Who?"

"He's one of the most faithful pro-lifers they have. And he's really nice. I found out today that he's a retired policeman, thirty-three years with the Bryan force. He stands at the exact same spot every Wednesday and Saturday morning for an hour, like clockwork. I don't think he's ever missed a day."

"How do you know so much about him?"

"Oh, we chat sometimes. Whenever he sees me he says, 'Hi, Abby, how are you today? I hope you have a wonderful day.' He's so sweet. He never bothers our clients at all, just takes his spot and greets everybody. Today it was burning up outside, and there he stood with an umbrella to keep the sun off him, just waving and greeting me like an old friend. He must be in his seventies, but no matter what the weather, he's out there, friendly as can be. You'd like him."

"I like him already," Doug answered. "Sounds to me like he's a faithful one. You haven't mentioned Marilisa lately. Is she still out there?"

"Oh yeah. She was there the other day. She's another one who's just so friendly. She was training a new volunteer. I've noticed that she and Shawn have quieted things down a good bit on their side of the fence. You know that lady with the awful enlarged photo of the aborted fetus that I've told you about?"

"Yes."

"Shawn took her aside one day last week and talked to her, and then she left. I haven't seen her since."

"Really? Hasn't she been coming since forever? What do you think that's about?" Doug asked.

"I've been getting the feeling that those Coalition people are trying to change the atmosphere at the fence, quieting the troublemakers. It seems to be working, too. And Shawn and Marilisa appear to be training volunteers to take the same friendly, conversational approach they use. It's changed a lot. I haven't seen the Grim Reaper for a long while, now that I think about it."

"You know, Abby, when you think of people like Marilisa and Mr. Orozco volunteering their time, does it ever occur to you that you might have a lot more in common with the Coalition people than you realize?"

"Yeah, right. We have one thing in common—the fence. But we're on opposite sides of it, remember?" After all, I reasoned, we were faced off at the fence. But I had to admit, when I watched Marilisa talk to clients, I often thought that she and I shared a bond of compassion for the women coming to our clinic. On the other hand, I'd heard rumblings about some kind of Coalition campaign.

I had no idea what was about to unfold.

CHAPTER SIX

40 Days and 40 Nights

The dynamic at the fence had been changing, thanks to enormous efforts by David, Shawn, and Marilisa along with other Coalition for Life supporters working behind the scenes. I only saw what happened at the fence. I was clueless about the extent of their other efforts. In August 2004, we discovered that the scope of those efforts had increased exponentially.

"Abby, guess who knocked on my door at home yesterday?" a clinic volunteer asked one day that month.

"Who?"

"Shawn Carney."

"Really? What on earth did he want?"

"It was the strangest thing. When I opened the door, we recognized each other. 'I know who you are,' I told him, and he recognized me, too. Then he said, 'We're just doing a simple campaign. We're asking people to pray for an end to abortion.'"

"He just came knocking on your door out of the blue and asked you to pray? That's it? What did you say?"

"I said, 'I can do that.' He thanked me and headed to the next house. One of my neighbors said it looked like he was going to every house in the neighborhood."

I later learned that the Coalition for Life canvassed 25,000 homes with that same simple request. I was impressed. In fact, as I went to bed that night, I felt a nudge to pray the same prayer myself. But I felt oddly conflicted. On the one hand, I should be happy to pray for an end to abortion. I wanted the number of abortions to decrease, right? But on the other, I didn't want abortion to end because I wanted women who felt they needed them to continue to be able to get them.

What would I have done and felt that night if I hadn't had two abortions myself? I couldn't imagine. For one thing, I'd have been the mother of two preschoolers, so I certainly wouldn't have been able to finish school—not if I had to work to support them and pay for housing and day care. What kind of future would I have had? No. I *needed* those abortions, right? Abortion was a necessary option.

A few days later, on September 1, the Coalition for Life launched the first-ever 40 Days for Life campaign. None of us—neither the clinic workers nor the pro-life volunteers—could have dreamed what God would set in motion through this campaign. Every hour, day and night, for forty days the Coalition posted volunteers at the fence. Inside the clinic, we peered out and discussed how well organized they were. Clearly this wasn't the same mismatched group we'd been seeing on abortion days. It was abundantly clear that now they were cooperating with each other. Their numbers had increased too—by a lot! They were working in shifts, with new folks arriving to relieve others like clockwork.

Many simply stood for their hour and prayed. Some approached the fence, but when they addressed patients, they spoke gently and offered literature or an invitation to come outside the fence to talk—no accusations, no nasty signs, simply a peaceful, prayerful force. And they consistently spoke words of welcome and kindness to us clinic workers. In fact, they were killing us with kindness.

Camera crews from the media soon showed up. That concerned us greatly because the women who come to a Planned Parenthood clinic don't want their pictures flashed on the nightly newscast. Even those who weren't coming for abortions might be coming for gynecological visits, birth control, and annual exams—all very personal, private matters. No one coming to or going from such an appointment would want an audience.

Some staff members at our clinic and at headquarters in Houston definitely seemed unhappy about the campaign. On the other hand, it presented Planned Parenthood with a fresh opportunity to publicly position itself. The usual Planned Parenthood talking points took on heightened language as if we were under siege, using phrases like "antiabortion protesters converging in demonstrations to harass our volunteers and clients." The police were called to the clinic a few times, and I was told their presence was needed to "protect" the workers and staff.

Once the early days of the 40 Days campaign were past and the TV camera crews gone, I was trying to figure out exactly why certain Planned Parenthood staffers felt so threatened by the campaign. I didn't like the feeling that we were surrounded by a 24/7 campaign either, but after all, it's not like they were firing guns or bombs at us—they were praying, for goodness' sake. How could that hurt? But the tension inside the clinic mounted. I was still just a part-time volunteer, so I reasoned that maybe the campaign was stressing the full-time workers in a way I couldn't quite grasp. After all, forty days and forty nights—those are biblical proportions! That's a long time to be surrounded nonstop by a large group of people who disagree with you but are so persistently . . . well . . . *nice* about it. It created an atmosphere I couldn't quite articulate.

As the campaign wore on, I tried to understand my mixed feelings about it. On the one hand, as a believer in God, how could I be unhappy about people praying? In fact, I wished I had the kind of prayer life some of the 40 Days for Life volunteers appeared to have—it seemed so real to them. My own efforts at prayer had been steadily drying up. I argued to myself that I should welcome these prayers. Many of the pro-lifers said things like "I'm praying for you today," and "I hope you have a peace-filled day" as I walked to and from my car.

On the other hand, I have to admit that I resented it. Clearly the implication was that God was on their side, not ours, and I vacillated between squirming in discomfort and feeling downright irritated at their arrogance. I considered myself a pro-choice Christian and knew lots of other people like me. I was helping people who needed help and, I believed, saving and improving lives. I didn't appreciate being surrounded and constantly watched by people who believed I was on the devil's side. After the first few weeks, I realized I was ticked off! Then at night I would chastise myself: What was the matter with me? How could I resent prayer?

When October 10, 2004, the last day of the 40 Days for Life campaign, finally rolled around, all of us at the clinic were relieved. But the irony was not lost on me: I was relieved that a *prayer* campaign was ending. Wasn't there something wrong with that?

Within six months of that first 40 Days for Life campaign, three very exciting things happened in my life. First, Doug proposed and I accepted. That same month, I was offered a part-time job at the Bryan clinic as a health-center assistant, working directly with patients for intake interviews and counseling women who had just learned they were pregnant. Four weeks later, I graduated from Texas A&M with my undergrad degree in psychology, and my position at the Bryan clinic was increased to full time.

I was thrilled! I'd studied and trained in psychology and counseling, and now I was doing it! I was sure this was what I was born to do. I now spent forty hours a week interacting with patients. I explained procedures and options, comforted, and counseled. I could see the difference I was making in women's lives, and I took that as proof of God's blessing.

Now that I was counseling women in crisis pregnancies, asking them if they wanted to see their ultrasound photo before making their final decision, I gave in to my own curiosity, which had surfaced under these new circumstances. I secretly looked up my own patient file and for the first time, laid eyes on the ultrasound photo of my own pregnancy taken the day of my medication abortion just over a year before. At eight weeks the fetus was quite small. As I studied the image, I was somewhat surprised to feel a deep sadness. I believed what I had been taught to believe—that the image showed a fetus and not a baby. But as I slid the photo back into the file, I choked back a wave of unexpected remorse.

"Mom," I announced into the phone one day after work, "you won't believe a case we had this week!" I was always eager to tell her something positive from the clinic. "A woman came in complaining of several physical problems. When we examined her, we discovered she had significant uterine cancer, and we got her to the ER for an emergency hysterectomy." I was overcome with the sense that God's hand had been present as we fought for this woman's life. I felt privileged to have been by her side, offering comfort and practical assistance. And I told myself that this situation justified the existence of our clinic and my role there.

Another day a woman came in who had recently been raped and now suspected she was pregnant. She was in such emotional pain. After confirming her fears through a pregnancy test, then listening to her and comforting her, I walked her through the three choices we presented when clients had an unwanted pregnancy: parent, place for adoption, or abort. In this case, after counseling, the woman decided on adoption. I connected her to a Christian adoption organization. They were able to link her up with a family. Accepting that the child had been conceived through sexual assault, the adoptive family not only gave the baby a wonderful home, but they extended tremendous support and love to the young birth mother herself. I found deep joy in being part of bringing such God-given healing to this wounded woman, another confirmation to me that God had me here for a purpose: to do His work in a broken world.

"I just know I'm here for a reason," I told Doug. "I share a mission with my coworkers to care for our patients. Several of us feel that way." But then I admitted I only felt that way when the woman chose not to abort. I found that odd, since I still believed that we needed legal access to abortion and that Planned Parenthood should offer it. Otherwise lives would be lost, or women would be hurt through botched abortions by unqualified providers. If that sounds more like talking points than a conversation between loved ones, you're right. Yet I repeated those talking points a good bit, as if hoping to convince my mom or Doug—or more likely myself—that the clinic was doing God's work.

"Abby, I know you love your job," Doug responded, "but do you really think you can separate what goes on there into two unrelated matters and pretend that the good done on the one hand cancels out the abortion on the other? Doing wonderful things doesn't balance out the ending of babies' lives. Your paycheck comes from those abortions, Abby. How do you reconcile that?"

I fumed. "We don't do any late-term abortions, Doug. We don't end the lives of babies. That's just misinformation—right-wing political propaganda! At the early stages, a fetus is just not viable outside the womb. Far better to remove fetal tissue early than to bring an unwanted baby into this world. Can you imagine where society would be today if all the abortions since *Roe v. Wade* hadn't happened? Besides, women have the right—the responsibility—to determine if and when they want to have a child." The debate was repeated more times than I can count.

I had two coworkers who were devout Catholics. One Monday they told me they'd heard an antiabortion sermon on Sunday. They confided to me that they felt the same way I did—that they were doing God's work except for abortion cases, and they talked about how they avoided any connection to the rooms where abortions were performed. We affirmed one another's thinking. In truth, nearly all of my colleagues worked in the clinic because of a sincere desire to help women—and many, like me, were drawn in spite of, not because of, abortion.

One day I counseled another woman who had been raped. Our counseling session was heartbreaking, and I agonized with her over her trauma. After vacillating back and forth, she chose abortion. I remember the depth of her weeping after it was over. In the months that followed, as she returned for checkups, we talked about her healing process. After several months, she felt that she was dealing with the rape fairly well.

"I was the victim. I completely understand that I carry no blame for the rape. But," she began weeping, "I keep having nightmares about the abortion. I feel so much guilt. I know I deliberately took the life of my child."

I tried to assure her that she'd made a difficult but understandable decision, but she looked back at me with absolute certainty and declared, "This is guilt I will carry the rest of my life." I couldn't help but feel guilt myself for the part I had played in her story.

I would discover over time that this was not uncommon. I've seen many women suffer emotional pain and guilt, often for years, over their decision to abort. In cases of rape, I found it particularly sad because often abortion seemed to add a new wound on top of the first.

During our engagement, Doug and I decided we wanted to make Sunday worship a regular part of our lives. I hadn't attended church regularly since I'd left home for college, and I longed to connect more deeply with God, especially after the 40 Days for Life campaign by the Coalition for Life. After visiting a few churches, we found one we both enjoyed. The service was contemporary, something new to both of us, given our conservative upbringings, and the sermons were stirring my heart. I was excited about becoming part of a church again. Even so, God still seemed distant. I would try to pray but often felt distracted. At times, I was afraid to pray—afraid that God would tell me to give up my job. I didn't want to give it up. I felt useful there.

On Sunday mornings I felt like a spiritual misfit, surrounded by people in touch with God while I just felt left out in the cold. But I wanted to belong—really belong—among other Christians. I was careful to avoid conversations about where I worked. Not that I was ashamed of where I worked, I'd tell myself, but I knew so many people wouldn't understand the good we did there. But it was impossible to avoid the subject entirely. Eventually word got around.

I didn't realize how significant that revelation would be.

After attending this church for several months, Doug and I decided we wanted to join. We mentioned it to one of the staff members, and the following week he approached us after the service. When I turned to give him a warm greeting, I could see that he felt awkward and uncomfortable.

"I talked to the pastor. He said that you are very welcome to attend here, but you won't be permitted to join."

"But—why not?"

"Because you work for Planned Parenthood. We are a pro-life church. We believe in the sanctity of human life."

I felt like I'd been punched in the stomach. "Are you telling me that even though I believe in Jesus as my Savior, I'm not welcome to join this church because of where I work?"

"You work at an abortion clinic, Abby."

I stood there, stunned, trying to process what he had just said.

"I'm really sorry," the man said. "We'd love to still have you attend."

I wanted to protest, but it was all I could do to hold back tears. Sensing my distress, Doug took my hand and led me out. Although we had loved attending that church, we could never bring ourselves to return after that.

While I realized the church took a pro-life stance, the pain of being rejected for membership ran deep. Since I believed I was doing the right thing for women in crisis, it had never occurred to me that I would be denied full participation in church for working at the clinic.

Doug and I discussed the situation at length and decided we would visit churches of other Christian traditions. Each week I'd anticipate and hope for a connection with God, a deep sense of His presence. But the sting of feeling rejected by that first church lingered. I couldn't push away the hurt and, increasingly, a sense of trepidation. Was God angry with me? Often, during times of congregational or silent prayer, I would freeze up, afraid to speak to God from my heart. I began to wrestle with an unspoken fear—one I dared not share even with Doug: What if I were going to hell because of my job?

As I revisit my journey now, I can't gain a clear picture of what I did with that thought. I remember having it, feeling troubled by it. But I don't recall any steps I took to resolve it. I didn't search God's Word for His will or seek counsel from other believers. As with so many other troubling thoughts, I let it pass out of my conscious awareness. I was leading an unexamined life, filled with inconsistencies.

From mid-2005 to mid-2006, life accelerated with lightning speed. Doug and I married. I notified Planned Parenthood that I planned to go to graduate school in Huntsville (about an hour from Bryan), and as I'd hoped, they invited me to transfer to the Huntsville

Planned Parenthood clinic as a part-time health-care assistant. We found a house in Huntsville and settled in, working during the days and attending school at night. It felt like a magical time, as if we were making our dreams come true. I was highly motivated at school, and I dreamed of climbing higher in the Planned Parenthood organization. The 2005 Lobby Day further reinforced my passion for the cause.

In Huntsville, Doug and I found another church where the preaching was challenging and the worship inspiring. With work and school, our schedules were full, so we didn't get involved beyond Sunday mornings, but we enjoyed being part of the congregation. I still felt more distant from God than I wished, but I also sensed the healing of time on the sting of that earlier church's rejection.

My work at the Huntsville clinic involved service and crisis intervention, which I found wonderfully rich and satisfying. As I moved closer to receiving my master's degree in counseling, a future at Planned Parenthood sounded more and more attractive to me. I traveled every other week to the Bryan clinic on abortion days to counsel women.

Both the Bryan and the Huntsville clinic were part of the same Planned Parenthood affiliate, Planned Parenthood of Houston and Southeast Texas, which encompassed twelve clinics, and I began paying more attention to news and happenings coming out of our headquarters in Houston.[5] During this time—probably because no abortions were performed at the Huntsville clinic—my worries over abortion quieted. In hindsight, I'm still baffled as to why that was, given that I commuted to Bryan every other Saturday to counsel women considering abortions. But it's the simple truth.

Doug and I were happy newlyweds immersed in school and

work. And then we discovered I was pregnant. There's an incredible irony in the fact that I had a career in educating women about contraception and yet, for the third time, conceived while using contraceptives. Doug was ecstatic. I was torn between intense joy and the shock of the unexpected. But my shock soon gave way to shared joy with Doug.

My memories of the day I confirmed my pregnancy are not among my most pleasant. Suspecting I was pregnant, I took a pregnancy test at work, and I didn't try to hide the news. When the test showed a positive result, there was a good deal of teasing. "You know, we can easily take care of that if that isn't the result you were hoping for," one colleague joked. I didn't find it funny. In fact, it hit much too close to home, shaking that deeply hidden box of secrets. It didn't help that several others made similar jokes before I left work that day.

Fortunately, sharing the good news with our parents is among the happiest memories of my life, with hugs and tears and laughter and great joy. Our parents, of course, believed this to be my first pregnancy, an impression I did not correct. But that knowledge tinged my happiness with a vague regret that I pushed aside and tried to forget.

I was excited the day of my first prenatal visit to my doctor. While filling out my initial paperwork, I came to a question asking how many pregnancies I had had. I remember wanting to lie and write that this was my first pregnancy because I felt ashamed. And then I felt guilty that I felt ashamed. Weird, I know, but typical of the odd seesaw of thought and emotion that characterized those years. In the end, I told the truth on that form about my previous abortions. It was the first time I had been honest about my abortion history on a medical form. A valuable lesson in dealing with clients during intake interviews—shame often holds patients back from revealing important medical history. I made a mental note that, going forward, I should circle back on the questions of history and do all I could to make my sessions with women feel safe to them so they'd be more likely to tell the truth, even if they did feel embarrassed by their responses.

In July 2006, when I was five months pregnant, I got a call from Cheryl. A position had opened up at the Bryan clinic, one that represented a considerable promotion: director of community outreach and health education. Though I still attended evening classes in Huntsville a few nights a week, the opportunity for a new challenge, one that offered a career path within the organization, was too good to pass up. I knew I'd love going out and developing community partnerships, working in public relations with the media, playing a role in preparations for Lobby Day and other rallies, and interacting with people in neighborhoods about the services we offered. And I was excited about working under Cheryl again. I respected her greatly and saw her as a career role model.

So I accepted the job and we moved back to Bryan. Doug was thrilled to land a job in his chosen field as a high school special education teacher. I assumed my new full-time role back at my home clinic. Of course, since I had come back to counsel on abortion days, I'd never truly been away. Now, however, I would be a leader there, and I was eager to make my mark.

CHAPTER SEVEN

The Code of Conduct

When I returned to the Bryan clinic, the face-off at the fence appeared far more peaceful than it had been at any time since I'd been involved with the clinic.

Unlike my early days as a volunteer escort, when the Grim Reaper raised his scythe and crudely lettered, accusatory signs bobbed up and down, the scene at the fence now reflected the prayerful, peaceful presence of the Coalition for Life. Through gentle yet persistent efforts, the Coalition had established a code of conduct for pro-life advocates coming to the fence that, with only rare exceptions, everyone honored. I respected this huge accomplishment on the part of the Coalition and felt that everyone—pro-life and pro-choice—had benefited. I knew that David Bereit and Shawn and Marilisa Carney had led that effort. And for that, they'd earned my respect. I still thought they were dead wrong ideologically, but I respected their good intentions.

Due to the nationwide interest in the Coalition's 40 Days for

Life campaign, David had moved to Washington, D.C., the year before my return to take on a national pro-life leadership role. Marilisa had become the director after David's departure. When she became a mother in January of 2006, just six months before my return, Shawn, her husband, assumed the role of director. I couldn't help but notice the parallels in Shawn's and my own track—in life as well as within our respective organizations. We'd both started as volunteers on opposite sides of the fence surrounding the Bryan clinic within thirty days of each other. He'd moved into a paid position around the same time I had, and now he had assumed the director's role a few months before I returned to the Bryan clinic as director of community outreach and health education.

I was now well into my second trimester, a fact that did not go unnoticed by the regulars at the fence upon my return. "Abby, you're expecting!" Marilisa called out when our paths first crossed after my return. "When are you due?" Even though I'd been at the Bryan clinic on abortion days for the previous six months, Marilisa hadn't seen me because when I'd visited the clinic on those days, she'd been home with her new baby.

When I saw her, my heart leapt. Marilisa had befriended me on my very first day as a volunteer. I'd believed her kindness and concern for me were genuine from the beginning, and everything I'd experienced since reinforced my instincts. Knowing she was a new mom gave me a common bond with her, since I was expecting too.

"Hey, Marilisa. It's good to see you." I strolled over to meet her at the driveway where the gate stood wide open. "I'm due in November, right around Thanksgiving."

"What a Thanksgiving you'll have! There is no greater gift than a child." From some other pro-lifer, that statement might have come off as a dig, but I knew that her comment was clearly an expression of her own joy in motherhood.

"I understand you had a little girl around Christmas. How is she?"

"Perfect! You should see Shawn with her. She's got him wrapped around her tiny little fingers already. He just beams when he holds her—like he glows in the dark!"

"I can imagine. I understand he's director of the Coalition now. How are things going? Any sign of the Grim Reaper?" I asked teasingly.

Marilisa grinned and rolled her eyes. "No, thankfully. Most everyone is very cooperative. We have the occasional new face who needs some coaching. There is one renegade named Jim—good intentions but bad methods. He's caused a lot of tension on both sides, even causing the police to get involved a few times. We've tried to reason with him, but we can't seem to control him." Marilisa shook her head.

I figured Cheryl would give me an earful about this Jim, and I was right. She told me she was particularly annoyed that some of the pro-lifers had been taking photographs of our younger clients and mailing them to their parents. Some of those parents then called the clinic, demanding to know what their daughters were doing there and threatening to sue.

When I told her that tactic didn't sound like something the Coalition for Life would do, I could tell she thought I was being naive. The pro-life rhetoric was heating up, she said, and so were the calls for violence. Then she pointed out our newly installed, upgraded cameras, which gave a 360-degree view of the clinic's driveway, parking lot, fence, and sidewalk.

Other security measures were in full force as well. At first, the precautions seemed excessive to me, but I had to admit that the pro-life movement had a lunatic fringe. Abortion doctors in several cities across the nation had been targeted, harassed, shot at, and had their homes and offices vandalized. The Internet chatter in support of such attacks was alarming. I didn't believe our clinic or doctors were at risk, but the idea that someone was taking photos of our clients' license plates was disturbing.

Cheryl, I thought at times, seemed to exaggerate the drama. I sometimes wondered if she did so because she really feared for our safety or because she wanted to rally support and camaraderie among our staff and volunteers, painting the picture of us as always under attack. But then we'd learn on the Internet of some new attack on an abortion clinic, and we'd all have a sense of heightened danger.

Our security practices reinforced the sense of being under attack. For instance (though this was nothing new), most of our abortion doctors arrived at the clinic with high drama. They would park in secret locations and be picked up by Planned Parenthood staff. On the ride to the clinic, they would hunker down in the backseat with a sheet over them. When the escort car arrived behind a privacy fence at our side entrance, often in the predawn darkness, the doctors would keep the sheet over their heads and scurry into the clinic as if they were being targeted by a sharpshooter.

Not all of our doctors went to these extremes. A few simply drove into our lot in their own cars and walked in the front door in broad daylight. I'd always found the high drama over the top, since anyone on the planet could go to the city hall of Bryan, do an open-records request, and find out the names of our doctors. But the drama fed the sense of siege inside our walls, which strengthened loyalty and support. There's nothing like opposition to solidify the troops.

I found it curious that paranoia was escalating, even though the scene at the fence had become considerably more peaceful.

In my new role I was trained as one of the few media relations contacts for our affiliate of twelve clinics in southeast Texas and Louisiana. Nothing seemed more important to the affiliate than preparing and sticking to our media talking points. I, in turn, trained our staff on the points to make when clients asked questions. During my training, I became aware not only of the importance of semantics but of the heavy influence the Planned Parenthood jargon had already had on my own thinking. I recall a slight feeling of having been . . . not duped, since I believed in the organization . . . but at least manipulated as a young recruit.

For example, it would have been accurate to refer to the prolifers at the fence on abortion days as advocates praying for an end to abortion while offering information to women on the brink of making a life-altering decision. That was not, however, the Planned Parenthood line. We were taught to refer to them—and think of them—as anti-choice extremists who would do and say anything to take away the rights of women and harass our clients. I find it disturbing now to look back and see how easily I adopted and used the talking points I was given. But, I reasoned, I was not there to represent myself. I represented Planned Parenthood. Besides, just as I was saying as spokesperson, we were a highly respected women's health organization dedicated to the education and reproductive health of women. We stood for women's rights and their free exercise of those rights—a cause I was proud to champion.

And I still deeply believed in the vision of the organization, perhaps more than ever before. I loved being back at the Bryan clinic and threw myself into my new role with a passion. I felt a greater sense of ownership for the clinic as a whole.

Meanwhile, Doug was enjoying his first months teaching, and we were preparing for the birth of our baby. The months seemed to fly by.

On November 16, 2006, I gave birth to a precious, healthy little girl. Doug and I named her Grace. The delivery was extremely difficult, resulting in some severe medical complications for me. I was forced to remain flat on my back in the days that followed and was unable to breastfeed or even pump breast milk. I had so anticipated the bonding experience of breastfeeding and was bitterly disappointed. Now my husband, family, and nurses took care of my baby's every need while I lay immobilized and helpless. A sense of loss and failure overtook me, leaving me filled with sadness and frustration rather than joy. Everyone assured me the feelings would pass, but even on the day we took Grace home from the hospital, a dark cloud hovered in my heart. I felt guilty for feeling that darkness. My mom came to stay with me, though, and I treasured her closeness.

I'd been working in a world of women for five years at this point. I believed I understood the bond that women shared with one another. But I was about to be initiated into a far deeper fellowship than I'd ever known. Motherhood is a powerful bonding force, and before I knew it, I was mysteriously woven into the fabric of this bond.

A few days after being released from the hospital, I received a call from a friend at the clinic. One of our colleagues had just lost her daughter in a car accident. I gasped in horror at the thought of losing a child. I empathized with her loss in a way I'd never have been able to empathize before.

As my friends from the clinic and I gathered over the next few days at the viewing and graveside, I sensed a bond, a sisterhood unlike anything I'd known before. We were like family, rallying around our friend who'd lost her child, supporting one another, contributing to help her meet the expenses she faced. We cried together and found a way to smile together as well. My colleagues shared in my joy of new motherhood and understood my tumultuous emotions in the aftermath of the birth. Never had I experienced such a deep level of connection with my coworkers. The simultaneous blending of my experience of becoming a mother, sharing the suffering of another mother in the death of her child, and witnessing the compassion of my coworkers for one another penetrated my heart. I carried these memories back with me to the clinic after my eight-week maternity leave, my sense of purpose at our clinic enhanced with deeper meaning.

Even so, I felt a deepening sadness. I was hopeful that plugging back into a church would jump-start my rebound from what I now assumed was a case of postpartum depression. We'd not yet found a church since returning to Bryan from Huntsville, and we both missed worshiping with fellow believers. This time we found a Baptist church that seemed to be a good fit. I avoided mentioning where I worked, hoping we wouldn't have a repeat of the rejection we'd experienced a few years before. It was good to be back in church, but God had never seemed more distant—a distance I longed to close.

In the months that followed I was aware that the deep sadness in my heart was not lifting. Perhaps the most alarming aspect of my dysfunction was that my emotional bond with Grace wasn't growing as I knew it should. And I felt helpless to change this. Logic would indicate that, as a trained therapist with a master's degree in counseling, I'd have known I needed medical attention for my worsening depression. Logic, however, seldom partners with depression. In my mind, I was a therapist and therefore *not* a patient.

Four people played a vital role in supporting me through this dark time and moving me toward the help I needed—Doug, my mom, and two very dear friends. One was a close friend from school, also a therapist, who was pregnant herself. The other friend was a coworker and trusted confidante, Valerie. I'd been there for her when her child had been seriously ill. Now she was there for me. It took months of urging from these four loved ones before I finally sought help from my doctor. I was fortunate—within thirty days of beginning to take an antidepressant, I was out of my depression and functioning fully once again. I couldn't believe I'd suffered so long so needlessly. Most important, my attachment to Grace quickly grew and deepened.

This personal experience with postpartum depression, though painful, would prove to be invaluable in the not-too-distant future.

My first words with Shawn Carney of Coalition for Life were probably just an exchange of hellos out by the fence over our first few years. But the first conversation I fully recall happened not terribly long after I'd given birth to Grace. The encounter left a strong impression.

Shawn was hosting a TV show for EWTN called *beingHUMAN*, a documentary series that chronicles the efforts of everyday people who are working to end abortion. The opening sequence of the series was filmed in the library of the Baptist church Doug and I were attending at the time. Most Baptist churches take a pretty strong stand against abortion, and yet there I was, working with Planned Parenthood and attending a Baptist church. I worried that Shawn knew I was attending this church, and I was afraid he would send a message to our pastor, something along the lines of, "Do you know that you have an abortionist attending your church?"

Considering what I knew of Shawn, just the fact that I felt such a fear shows that I had bought into some of the paranoia Planned Parenthood seemed to encourage. But it was also true that, since being back at the Bryan clinic, I'd already experienced a few frightening incidents. Some of my neighbors and people in our community had gotten letters from a man who identified me by name and likened what I was doing at Planned Parenthood to molesting a child. The same man had sent out similar letters about other Planned Parenthood staffers and the doctors who performed abortions at our clinics. Several of us suspected that it was Jim, the pro-lifer the Coalition had been unsuccessfully struggling to influence toward constructive rather than destructive methods.

Shawn, I knew, was a good guy who wouldn't purposely damage my reputation. Still, given the horrible letters and the pain of the former church rejection, I was concerned. So I approached Shawn at the fence one day and said, "I hear you've been filming over at my church. I know you have good intentions, and I know you think you're doing the right thing. But I'm pro-choice. There are other people at my church who are pro-choice—I'm not the only one. My church has no problem with my working here. In fact, I have a lot of supporters there."

I know it was a foolish way to handle it. I'd actually kept quiet at my church about my job. But a few people there knew what I did, and news gets around, though I doubted the pastor knew.

Shawn smiled. "I think of that as a pretty pro-life church. But you know, just because you have a few people there who agree with you doesn't make it right. Even if everyone agreed, it wouldn't make it right." Then he promised he wouldn't mention me or my job to the pastor or anybody else there. He suggested I not talk about it either.

I remember thinking as I walked away, *He didn't know I went there? I should have kept quiet. But it sounds like he won't tell anyone.*

And he didn't. In fact, as I discovered later, he felt some concern for me after that conversation. He knew my church well enough to know that it was predominantly pro-life, and he was afraid that if I went around talking about my pro-choice beliefs, I'd get thrown out of my own church. He had no idea, of course, that I'd already been through a similar experience and hoped to never feel that rejection again.

My experience with depression reminded me of how much I loved working directly with patients. Though I was enjoying the role of director of community services, I deeply missed working directly with women in crisis. Cheryl must have sensed it. She had been promoted to regional medical services director for our affiliate and recommended I apply for the job of director of the clinic. Knowing she felt I was up to the task was a huge boost to me. I decided to take the leap.

"Hey, Mom—big news today. Cheryl is encouraging me to apply to be director of the clinic."

"Abby, have you thought about the fact that, as the director, you'd actually be in charge of the abortions in your clinic? Do you see that as different from counseling women about their choices?"

I was frustrated—partly at my mom but mostly at myself for inviting this conversation. How had I expected her to respond? "Mom, as director I can do even more to bring abortion numbers down. I can make ours the best clinic in the affiliate, increase our education services, build a closer connection to adoption services, and draw in more clients for contraception to decrease the number of unwanted pregnancies. This is an opportunity to really make some changes."

She didn't sound convinced. "Abby, what do you want me to say? You tell me how bad it makes you feel when people don't like what you do. You're even afraid to tell people at your church what you do for a living. But many people don't like abortion. *I* don't like abortion. I'm proud of your capabilities and accomplishments, but I can't pretend to like your choice of career."

Later that evening, I tried a new thought out on Doug: "I'm going to pray that if I'm not supposed to be working at the clinic, I won't get the promotion."

He looked thoughtful. "You applied for the job already, right?"

"Yeah."

"So you're asking God to show His will by stopping something you've already set in motion?"

"Well, God can intervene. If I pray that way and still get the job, I'll know it's God's will that I run the clinic."

Doug didn't look any more convinced than my mom had sounded. But I told myself this plan made sense. *I do want God to show me if He wants me out.*

"Dear God," I prayed later than night, "if You don't want me at Planned Parenthood, please don't let me get the promotion. Amen."

The next day I got the promotion.

I'd been naively stepping closer and closer to darkness and further and further from the light for several years by then. I've since owned up to the fact that if I had truly been seeking God's will, I would have been reading the Bible and spending time in concentrated prayer, listening for His wisdom. I would have been seeking the counsel of spiritually mature believers rather than hiding my livelihood from them.

Instead, I made a childish bargain. In so doing, I thought I won. I accepted the job and cheerfully celebrated that God had blessed my career move. In reality, I lost. Because now, as my mother had pointed out, I had taken upon my shoulders the mantle of responsibility for everything that happened in that clinic.

CHAPTER EIGHT

My Enemy, My Friend

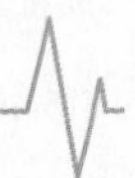

I WAS SURPRISED HOW READY I FELT for my first week as director of the Bryan clinic. There were so many changes I was eager to make, and I didn't want to waste a day getting started. I was ready to roll. The first major change was one I would not announce. I would model it instead. I was determined to build a positive, cooperative relationship with the Coalition for Life.

"I've made a vow about something at the clinic," I told Doug as I dressed for my first day as director.

"A vow? About what?"

"I vow never to call the police on the Coalition—unless, of course, someone is violent or lighting a fire or actually damaging property. But if anything like that happened, it wouldn't be the Coalition anyway. That would be some troublemaker they have no control over."

Doug smiled. "That *will* be a change. Seems to me the clinic has always called the police for every little thing. I'll bet the police hate it when your clinic calls."

"I think you're probably right. But I'll call them in for real crimes only. If a problem comes up with the Coalition, I'll just call Shawn and discuss it with him." I told Doug I wanted to build a strong relationship between the community and the clinic and get rid of the adversarial distrust. It's not like either of us had a secret agenda. They believed in wiping out abortion; we believed in reducing unwanted pregnancies and protecting a woman's reproductive rights. But I'd watched them at the fence for a long time. I was convinced they cared about these women, just like we did.

"Sometimes I think we have more in common than we do differences," I told him. "It's just that our differences are so . . . well . . . drastically different!" I was on my soapbox.

"Okay, Abby. You go single-handedly change the nature of the pro-life/pro-choice battleground. I've got students to teach." He kissed me good-bye and left. I finished going over some details with Grace's new nanny and cuddled my daughter for a few more minutes before heading in to work.

I didn't have to wait long before testing my new approach. One of the staff came to me that week and said, "Abby, I have another client complaining about the camera out front."

"Ours or the Coalition's?"

"Theirs. She's asking me if they plan to show the pictures someplace, revealing that she came here."

"Okay. I'll talk to the Coalition about it."

We had our cameras mounted along our fence. The Coalition for Life's practice for some time had been to set up a manned camera and tripod each day. As I understand it, there had been a lawsuit long before between a clinic worker and a pro-lifer, and ever since, the cameras were there. There had been times when a pro-lifer was overly aggressive with the camera, following us closely or sticking it in our faces as we walked. I'd seen Coalition volunteers, including Shawn, put a stop to such tactics, as this was not their style, but a few zealots occasionally misbehaved. Today this was not the case. The pro-lifers' camera was properly resting on its tripod next to our driveway.

I was actually glad to have an opportunity to test out my new face-to-face approach, with no police involved. Here was my chance.

I looked out the window and saw Shawn. *Guess I'll just tackle this head-on.* I went outside and walked over to Shawn, who was standing out by the fence.

"Shawn, some of our clients find your camera intimidating. Is there some way you could move it out of sight?"

He seemed sympathetic. "I can understand that. But unfortunately, it's necessary. It's not just for our protection; it's for yours as well. If anything were to happen, there's a photographic record."

I shook my head. "Shawn, you don't need to protect *us*. We have our own cameras. Look—can you at least move your camera to the other side of the driveway so it's a little farther away? It wouldn't be as obvious that way, and maybe our clients wouldn't be so afraid they could be identified. That's their fear. They're concerned someone is filming for the purpose of revealing their identities."

He shook his head. "Can't do it. We need a good angle on what's actually happening here at the fence. If there were ever any questions, we'd need it to be clear."

"It's just such a personal and vulnerable decision for many of our clients to come here—they have parents or husbands or boyfriends or coworkers or friends who have no idea they are pregnant or need medical attention or contraceptives. So the last thing they want to worry about is the fear of a video in someone's hands that shows them walking into our clinic."

My patience was getting a little thin at this point. I was trying hard to find some compromise, to work with them, to keep things positive and conciliatory, and it seemed to me that Shawn wasn't working with me.

When it was clear I wasn't getting anywhere, I turned to head back into the clinic. But I'd only taken a step or two when I turned back to him and said, "You know—" He looked taken aback, as if he thought I was going to get nasty. But I just thought he should see our point of view. "There have always been people like us—like Planned Parenthood—defending the rights of women and human rights in general. Isn't that what the emancipation movement was about in the 1800s, and then in the early 1900s, the suffrage movement? In World War II, people tried to stand up for the Jews. And now there are people like us, standing up for the reproductive rights of women, just as the suffrage movement stood up for their voting rights."

He listened respectfully, and then he simply said, "Abby, you don't have to justify your job to me."

What? *Justify* my job? "I'm not justifying, " I said. "I just want to explain—"

"And you don't have to explain what you're doing either. The truth is, you just cited two instances of injustice—the slaves and the Jews—that could only exist because a whole segment of our population was dehumanized. Society's acceptance of that is what allowed injustice to continue. And that's exactly what Planned Parenthood does to the unborn."

I was speechless. It wasn't that I couldn't have come back with a thoughtful response. I could have. But there was such a simple, straightforward logic to what he said. I looked away from him for a moment or two to process his words.

Then I looked back at him. Shawn would tell me a few years later that he remembered that I put my hand on my hip, and he wasn't sure what I would say—he thought I looked as if I were about to light into him. But all I said was, "You aren't going to convert me." And I turned and went back into the clinic.

Shawn says he chuckled as I walked away, amused by my defiance. But he also began praying for me immediately. He believed I would not have said what I said about his converting me if I hadn't, at some level, considered it a possibility.

It wasn't quite the new start with the Coalition for Life I had in mind.

In my first weeks as director I wanted to set some new best practices. One of the first was to emphasize to my staff that the reason we were here was to help our clients. For instance, I reminded them that if our posted hours said we were open until 4:30, we didn't lock the door until 4:30, even if that meant we'd be there until 6:00. "We are a service organization," I said again and again. Also, on very quiet days, I would send staff out to put up flyers at apartment complexes, Laundromats, and the A&M campus to get the word out about our free annual exams, Pap smears, and birth control. We didn't have the money to advertise, but flyers were inexpensive.

"Let's decrease those unwanted pregnancies," I'd remind the staff. "If a patient comes in for any service, make sure you ask about their use of contraception. We need to be advocates for the cause." Now that I was director, I was beginning to learn about our financial reports and was surprised to discover that we sometimes lost money on the family planning side of our business. Because our clinic did abortions and because those abortions were lucrative, our bottom line seemed okay to me. I knew we got grants from a government title funding source and that most of our clients' contraceptive and testing bills were partially paid by government funding, but I discovered that often those funds covered only half of the expenses. We had to make up the difference by charging the clients, but if they didn't have the resources, my clinic provided the service anyway. After all, we weren't in the business of making money. We were a service provider for the good of the community. Or so I thought. So in spite of the loss, I stressed to my staff that we were to reduce the number of abortions by reducing the number of unwanted pregnancies, and that meant proactively advocating contraception to our clients.

Also critically important to me was informed consent about the medical risks of procedures, especially about medication abortions.[6] I'll confess I had a pet peeve about those. Remembering the horrible experience I'd had with my own, I urged the staff to make sure that, when counseling clients, they clearly emphasized the severe side effects of RU-486, especially for patients who were past week six or seven. Many women seemed to think that by choosing a medication abortion, they'd have more control and wouldn't be subjected to anesthesia or surgical risks. Or perhaps they believed a medication abortion would be easier to hide from their families. After all, perhaps they thought they could just complain about having a bad menstrual cycle rather than needing a recovery period. But that wasn't true. Many women called us back, thinking they were dying because the cramping or bleeding was so intense. And I wondered how many other women, like me, never called, choosing instead to suffer in silence.

If a client insisted on a medication abortion, I told my staff, they should let them know it might be bad—really bad. I didn't want any surprised patients. I asked them to talk patients out of the procedure if they were past seven weeks. Beyond that point, too many attempts failed. Finally, I told my staff to make sure the women agreed to come back for the mandatory four- to fourteen-day follow-up and ultrasound so we could verify that the uterus was empty. Don't give up if they don't return, I told them. Keep calling. I became increasingly concerned about the number of medication abortion patients who had to return for a surgical abortion because the medication abortion didn't completely work.

One day I was at the front intake counter when a girl in her twenties came in carrying a little bag with four pills in it.

"I'm pregnant," she told me. "I need to have an abortion, but I don't have any money, so I'm going to take these pills. I know you can't give me any advice or anything, but I need you to tell me when I would need to go to the emergency room."

"Whoa, whoa, I can't let you do that," I insisted. "You have no idea how seriously wrong this could go. And where did you get those pills? How do you know what they are?"

"They're abortion pills. I'm supposed to take four, but I can't tell you where I got them. I've got to have this abortion, and I don't have any money."

"I don't want your money. But there are risks, possible complications. . . . I'd rather do an abortion for free and make sure you're safe."

It took a while, but I finally talked her into setting up an appointment for a few days later. She was at six weeks and wanted a medication abortion, so it was performed. A week and a half later she returned for her follow-up, but her ultrasound now showed that she was seven and a half weeks. The medication abortion hadn't worked. The fetus was still alive and growing! Good cardiac activity, apparently healthy.

"Well, maybe this is sign from God," she said. "Maybe I should have the baby." Her clinician freaked out, trying to explain the risk of damage and complications to the fetus from the failed abortion pill. But there was no changing the young woman's mind. She insisted that this was a sign she was to have the baby. She left, and we never heard from her again. We have no idea what happened to her or the baby.

With my new "never call the police" policy, it seemed that tensions between the clinic workers and the Coalition for Life continued to decrease—except when it came to Jim or a few others like him. Every now and then, he or someone with similar tactics would resurface, and trouble came with them. From where I stand now I can imagine that Jim, like many other zealots on either side of an issue, believed that extreme actions win victories for their "side." In truth, everything Jim did for the cause of life instead fed the strength and resolve of the pro-choice side. Even as a believer in women's right to choose, I hated to see such actions strengthen the cause of abortion, and that is precisely what they did.

At the end of one hard day at the clinic, I climbed into my car and spotted a note on my windshield. When I opened it, I felt a flash of anger followed by a foreboding anxiety. It was a typed death threat, promising to do to me what we at the clinic did to babies. Two other threats followed within a few weeks, one mailed to my home, one to the office. One of them read, "It's too bad that Grace won't have a mother." That one sent me over the edge.

This was a situation for the police, who in turn called the FBI, the Department of Justice, and the U.S. Marshals office. Law enforcement sent the notes off so that fingerprints and DNA evidence could be collected, but in the end they came up empty. It was a horrible ordeal. Planned Parenthood, concerned for my safety, had cameras and a security system installed at my house.

Not long after, Jim was spotted at the clinic taking pictures of the license plates of our clients. I called the police. When I went out for lunch that day and climbed into my car, Elizabeth, one of the regular Coalition for Life workers who was always friendly, called out a greeting to me through the fence. The timing wasn't good. She had a young volunteer with her I'd not seen before. I later learned her name was Heather. I stepped out of the car, slammed the door, and marched over to the fence. My frustration and anger must have been clear—I heard Heather, whose eyes were wide open in apprehension, say, "Oh no, what's she going to do?"

"Why do you associate with people like Jim?" I demanded. "Don't you know he hurts your cause? His crazy antics make the pro-choice people furious with all of you. He solidifies your opposition against you. Get him out of here and keep him away! He dirties all your efforts!" I turned on my heel, jumped into my car, slammed the door again, and took off.

"Good morning, Abby! Beautiful day today, isn't it? Isn't the sunshine wonderful?"

"Hey there, Mr. Orozco. Yes, it is." *Must be Wednesday,* I thought. Dear Mr. Orozco, did he *ever* miss a day? I couldn't think of a Wednesday or Saturday morning since I'd arrived in 2001 that he hadn't been there. I headed into the clinic ready for a typical day. It turned out not to be typical at all.

As director, I didn't counsel patients except in unusual cases. This day, however, a staff member came into my office. "There's a woman I think really needs you. All she'll say is that she has to talk to someone. She's deeply distraught."

After I'd spent a few minutes with this woman, she began pouring out her story. Her sister, she said, had caught her trying to smother her own baby. As she talked, sobs wracked her body. Her shame, guilt, and hopelessness came pouring out—her emotional deadness toward her child, her sense of isolation and despair. I recognized nearly every emotion and twisted thought process that I'd suffered during my own postpartum depression. My heart broke for her and with her, and in that moment I knew that if there was a reason I'd had to go through the dark time, it was so that I could help this woman, this mother whose depression had deepened so badly that she'd become a danger to herself and her child.

When she finally quieted, I looked into her eyes. "There aren't many times in life when someone can say to us, 'I know exactly how you feel.' But I'm telling you that I do know how you are feeling."

"Really? Have you gone through this too?" She seemed to relax with relief.

"I have. We are going to help you. We can't do it alone, but you need to trust me. Can you do that?"

She agreed. I made a few calls, then took her to the hospital where we met a crisis team. While they worked with her, I made out a report to Child Protective Services. I had already told her I would do this and that she'd be given the resources, training, and medication she needed to enable her to get her child back and be a strong parent. This is truly one of the most meaningful success stories of my lifetime. The woman was able to recover from her depression and parent her child. She thrived. And I knew that had I not walked through my own darkness, I would have been so appalled when I heard of her attempt to smother her child that I wouldn't have been able to reach out, empathize, and help. I now treasure that time I spent in the darkness, and thank God for using it.

One friendly face at the fence, Elizabeth, was incredibly persistent in her efforts to befriend me. I realized that the Coalition for Life had "targeted" me as someone they hoped to win over to their side through kindness and friendship. I didn't mind that. I believed they really cared about the women coming into the clinic, just as I did, and we had come to a place of mutual respect. I also believed they were wrong, of course—but well-meaning and sincere.

I pulled up to work one day and saw Elizabeth holding a bouquet of flowers. I was totally freaked out. I knew they were for me, but I could not bring myself to accept them over the fence. My coworkers would think that was crazy! I was totally nervous at the thought of pulling into my usual spot by the fence, as she'd hand me the flowers in plain sight of everyone. But I knew Elizabeth wasn't going anywhere, so I pulled up right by the back door instead of my usual spot. I thought maybe I could quickly run in as if I had some urgent need to attend to and she wouldn't be able to talk to me.

But she called out. I heard her say she had brought the flowers for me. I just sprinted in the door and acted as if I didn't hear her. I felt really bad. We weren't friends, but I felt like I had betrayed her. It was a strange feeling. I remember going to my office and watching her out the window. She looked so sad and disappointed. After about thirty minutes, she went to the center of the driveway and laid the flowers right in the middle. I couldn't believe it! I had hoped she would just take them with her. Now there they sat.

I didn't want them to get run over, so I made up the excuse

that I needed to go empty the trash can. I hurriedly picked up the flowers—beautiful lilies—on my way to dump the trash. Tucked inside was a handwritten card: *The Lord has done great things for us, and we are filled with JOY. Psalm 126:3. I'm praying for you, Abby!* I could imagine Elizabeth picking out the bouquet and writing the note. I was deeply touched. I carried them gently inside, put them in water, and displayed them in the break room for about a week. I carried the card back into my office and tucked it in the front of my little desktop cardholder that held various other thank-you notes and articles to read.

Whether I was a "project" or not, I saw Elizabeth's gift as a genuine act of friendship. I had no idea how her thoughtfulness and prayers would one day serve a far greater purpose than to brighten my day.

Another 40 Days for Life campaign began in September 2007. By now we'd become accustomed to them. The Coalition for Life held one every fall and every spring. But this fall the Coalition people were positively beaming with excitement. The reason? David Bereit was launching the same campaign they'd started here in eighty-nine cities simultaneously across the country.

Here in Bryan I didn't think I'd ever seen their numbers stronger. Elizabeth filled me in when I went out for lunch that day. "Have you heard we exceeded our goal of participating cities?" she asked. We had an audience; praying people lined the fence. The campaign was in full swing.

"How many?" I asked

"We were aiming for twenty. Abby, we've got eighty-nine cities! And this is just our first year to go national! We've been training the leaders through webcasts—how to deal with the media, how to befriend clinic workers and not see them as the enemy." She paused a moment, realizing how I might take that.

I just laughed heartily. "Well, you could sure teach that well! Look at us, huh?" How could I feel threatened by that? I liked having her as my "fence friend." In fact, I would have enjoyed a trip to the coffee shop—but I wasn't sure my staff would understand.

Elizabeth and I had no idea that day of the victory she was about to enjoy—not a victory of friendship, but a victory of two lives saved.

A young woman came into the clinic that week, asking for a pregnancy test. But before she made it to the front door, Elizabeth caught her attention at the fence. They spoke for a while, then the girl came inside. Her test was positive, and she opted for abortion. She went into the back to have her ultrasound.

"Twins? Twins!" I was in the hallway passing the examination room when I heard the girl's exclamation. "I'm gonna have twins? I can't believe it. I can't abort twins!"

That isn't unusual. In my experience, many times when a woman discovers she is pregnant with twins, she decides not to abort. It's fascinating how two heartbeats rather than one makes the human life within seem more real.

In no time at all, the girl was getting dressed. "I've got to go tell that lady at the fence! She won't believe it. She said she was going to pray for me. I hope she's still out there."

She was. Elizabeth had been waiting, eyes glued to the front door, for the girl to return, wondering if the test would be positive and, if so, hoping she'd be able to persuade her not to abort. The girl burst out the front door and literally ran toward Elizabeth and threw her arms around her. "I'm having twins!" she called out.

People at the fence clapped and cried out, "Praise God!" It turned into a party. Someone offered a camera, and soon the girl and Elizabeth were posing in front of the clinic. As it turned out, the girl was from another city, where her father was a pastor. She decided to tell her parents what had happened. I learned later, through the Coalition for Life, that before giving birth, she decided to allow her twins to be adopted by a loving family, and she and her parents formed a strong bond with the adoptive family.

I know how much it meant to the Coalition for Life that this event happened during a 40 Days for Life campaign. I celebrated it, too, because after all, I believed adoption was a wonderful option, and I had always preferred adoption over abortion. I saw this as a victory for the cause I believed in—reducing the number of abortions.

With all the prayers encircling us during that campaign, I couldn't help but wonder how they might be affecting what was happening on our side of the fence.

CHAPTER NINE

Irreconcilable Differences

SHE WAS A TINY WOMAN, so petite I wondered if she was a size 2. I don't think I'd ever seen such a muscular abdomen. She had scheduled an abortion, so the clinician began with a routine pelvic exam. That's when I got called back.

"I was doing her pelvic exam, and, Abby, something kicked me back."

"I saw her come in. She's not even showing. How can she be far enough along for you to feel a kick?"

"That's why I called you back here. I want you to help with the ultrasound."

And sure enough, this tiny little lady was not only pregnant, she was a full thirty-six weeks along! We were all amazed, but none more than she. She said she had no idea. She really thought she was only seven weeks, and, judging by her size, that would have been a reasonable guess. We explained to her that an abortion was out of the question. We did, however, call a Christian adoption agency I'd been in contact with previously. They were wonderful. This was a story with a happy ending. When she gave birth, the baby was placed in the arms of a loving family who'd been waiting many years for a child.

I wish all the late-term pregnancies we saw had happy endings. Sadly, they didn't, and these were, for me, the most painful cases of all.

The first time I ever encountered a woman seeking a late-term abortion left me shaken. She, too, was petite, but with a big, full, pregnant belly. She looked like she could give birth at any time. I happened to be filling in at the front desk when she walked in.

"I'd like to schedule an abortion, please."

I did a double-take. Her tone of voice was as nonchalant as if she'd just ordered a Big Mac. I ushered her to the back where we could talk privately and asked her to talk to me about why she'd come in.

"I just found out that I'm pregnant, and I've just got to get this thing out of me. I feel like I have an alien inside me." I was so taken aback I was speechless. I spent some time listening and asking questions, doing an intake interview, and trying to get a handle on the real story. Though I found her perspective shocking, she seemed fully cognizant of the facts. Yet somehow she truly seemed not to have realized she was pregnant until quite recently, and no matter how far along she was, she wanted that baby aborted.

Notice I said *baby*, not fetus. If there were any absolutes in my perspective on abortion, this was one: I was vehemently opposed to late-term abortions when the baby was viable outside the womb. On that point I had been immovable from the start. A baby is currently considered viable at twenty-one to twenty-four weeks. At the Bryan clinic we did abortions up to fourteen weeks, and at the time, our Houston office did them up to sixteen weeks. An ultrasound revealed this woman's baby was at twenty-three weeks.

I explained to her that abortion was not an option for her at Planned Parenthood.

She would not be thwarted in her goal. "Then where can I get this thing taken out of me?"

I was in what felt an impossible situation at that moment. At our clinic, when a client wanted a late-term abortion, we referred them to a medical clinic where that could be done. I knew I had to give her the referral information, but I didn't want to. I knew her baby was viable outside the womb—where I drew the line for abortions—and I wanted to find a way to break through to her, hoping she would reconsider. So first, I told her about how wonderfully adoption works out for many families. I described the process and the agencies we worked with. She made it clear she was not interested. Finally, I very clearly described a late-term abortion procedure, doing my best to help her see it was a horrible procedure, but she was unmoved.

"Yeah. I know how it's done. I don't care. I've just got to have this abortion."

"Do you understand," I continued, "that at your point of twenty-three weeks, your baby is actually viable outside your womb?"

"I figure it's all the same, you know? Six weeks or twenty-three weeks, it's all the same."

But it's not, I wanted to say. *It's not the same at all. This is a baby now!* But all I could do was give her the referral information.

That night I ranted about it to Doug. "I just couldn't believe how casual she was about it! I feel sick about it. Just sick. How can she say it's the same whether the pregnancy is six weeks along or twenty-three? That's just ludicrous!"

I couldn't have given Doug a bigger opportunity to challenge my thinking, and he did! We argued at length that night, Doug trying to open my eyes to the fact that a human life, whether only six weeks along or not, was just as worthy of life as the twenty-three-week-old baby I now wanted to protect. I, on the other hand, was incensed that he'd lump me in with late-term abortionists, as if what we did at our clinic was comparable to what they did.

But I wouldn't budge. Neither could I let go of the sense of being an unwilling party in her decision.

If the scenario over my response to the late-term abortion isn't evidence enough of my deep-seated inconsistency, my relationship with Dr. George Tiller paints an even clearer picture. Dr. Tiller was a well-known abortionist in Wichita, Kansas. I'd met him several times at National Abortion Federation meetings and liked him immensely. I found him to be a warm, caring man. Very friendly. I had a number of conversations with him and truly enjoyed his company. At conventions I'd see him give friends great big bear hugs, listen to others intently, and offer encouragement and support.

But he was well-known for performing late-term abortions. I remember watching him interact with others at a conference one time, and wondering how such a kind man, such a good man, could kill a twenty-four-week-old baby. He was a grandfather. How could he stand the ugliness of the procedure, and how did he justify it to himself? It troubled me.

As I look back at myself at this point in my journey, I am baffled as to how I could wonder about his ability to justify himself when I felt no need to justify myself for working in an abortion clinic while telling myself I was a champion of decreasing abortions. I see the frustration and anger I felt over the woman who decided to abort at twenty-three weeks—a decision I abhorred because her child was viable—yet I also see myself chatting comfortably with a man who performed that procedure countless times. Somehow

I managed to hold these irreconcilable perspectives with no need to resolve them.

Self-deception is a powerful force.

So is confession.

In early 2008 Doug and I began attending an Episcopal church. I'd grown weary of trying to avoid discussions of my job at our Baptist church, and my longed-for sense of connection to God was still eluding me. In fact, it seemed to me that the distance between me and God was growing. I knew the Episcopal church was pro-choice, and I welcomed the idea of no longer hiding my career on Sunday mornings. Doug and I, having never been part of a liturgical church, were both intrigued by the beauty and practice of the worship service.

From our very first visit I was particularly moved by reciting the confession of sin. "Most merciful God, we have sinned against you in thought, word, and deed," we would pray, followed by a moment of silence. There was only one problem. Every week, when we came to that part of the service, I felt a battle within. I found myself wanting to confess my part in abortion, yet I also argued against it.

The internal wrestling match I'd tried to avoid for years had, since becoming the clinic director, been intensifying. And yet, rather than wanting to flee the liturgy with its public confession of sin, I was drawn to it. I sensed that I was nearing God, and I wanted that, even though I squirmed in discomfort for fear that God disapproved of my job. Week after week I'd struggle, believing on the one hand that I was doing God's work by helping women in need and yet fearful of discovering that God might want me to leave a career I was enjoying—a career I saw as a meaningful way to make a difference in the world for good.

I recall one evening in 2008 when that argument with myself startled me. Our Planned Parenthood affiliate employed a security director who kept all our clinics informed about security threats in Texas as well as nationwide clinic security issues, pro-life events, and the like. She'd managed to get herself on the e-mail list for Coalition for Life and always forwarded the messages to Cheryl and me.

This particular evening I was checking e-mail at home while Doug and I were each sitting at our computers. I opened their newsletter and found myself a bit put out. The Coalition for Life had just had their big annual spring banquet. I couldn't believe it. They'd not only filled 1,500 seats, they had turned people away because of an overflow crowd. According to their newsletter, they'd raised $300,000 that night.

"Doug, do you believe this? Fifteen hundred people! And last February I couldn't even pull in two hundred to *our* donor banquet. When I asked the affiliate headquarters to allow me to try again this year, they refused to finance it at all."

"That's quite a turnout, all right," he answered, not looking up from his computer.

A disturbing thought surfaced and I couldn't help but voice it. "Doug, do you think it's likely that 1,500 people could be wrong?"

Doug looked up and grinned at me. "Probably not about this. Not too likely." And he returned to his work. I squirmed a bit as I thought about the community rallying around Coalition for Life and distancing itself from Planned Parenthood. It wasn't a good feeling.

Despite bouts of conscience and guilt, I saw a steady stream of women in need of compassionate assistance, and I was proud of working with a staff who cared about them. I wanted to do all I could to enhance the services we offered. I learned of a rape crisis center not far away and decided to attend one of their training sessions. I was impressed, particularly with how they counseled women who'd become pregnant through rape, so I invited one of their trainers to come to our clinic to provide training for us.

We closed our clinic for half a day, and the trainer offered our staff great insights into the perspectives and needs of women who'd been brutalized in this way. She was a huge proponent of adoption and discussed how giving a child to a waiting, loving family often brought deep healing to women who'd been raped. I resonated so deeply with her advice because of some of the women I'd encountered. When that day ended, I felt I'd made an important and life-giving contribution to our clinic's impact on our community.

There were two coworkers with whom my working relationship was quickly developing into meaningful friendship. One was Megan. She was a nurse-practitioner who consistently demonstrated deep compassion and gentleness toward our clients. We began having lunch together and soon were close friends. Another was Taylor. She was a teenager, a bit timid, and I soon found myself feeling a bit like a mother hen, working to build her confidence. I appreciated what Cheryl had done to coach and encourage me, and I wanted to follow in those steps and do the same kind of mentoring.

My love for my work, my appreciation for the staff, and my belief in our good purpose spilled over one day into a decision to add some beauty to our building. I had never forgotten how, on my very first day as a volunteer, our fence had reminded me of a prison. So one day I showed up at the office with some gardening tools and flowers and planted flowers along the fence. The Coalition for Life volunteers seemed to appreciate them as well, and over the next few weeks quite a few of them complimented us.

One day while tending the flowers I overheard one of the young volunteers who had become a regular. His name was Bobby.

"That's Abby," I heard him quietly explain to one of their new recruits. "I call her the Motivator. She's the clinic director, but you'll notice that she really is sincere and cares about everybody. I've seen her offering her volunteers umbrellas to keep the sun off and making sure everyone is drinking water on hot days. And she's usually friendly to us, too. But don't cross her!" I couldn't help but smile.

Bobby quickly became a favorite among our staff, especially our newly recruited volunteer escorts. He could strike up conversations with anyone, and no sooner would he show up at the fence than I'd spot one of our volunteers hanging out over there, just shooting the breeze with him. He had one of those open faces that just welcomes you in.

"Oh my word!" I heard a coworker gasp. She was standing by one of the front windows facing the fence.

"What is it?" I asked her.

"A nun. There is a nun in full habit standing in the driveway."

I walked over to the window to look, and soon several of us were gawking out the window. The temperature was near 100 degrees that day, yet there in the hot sun was a nun dressed in a heavy, dark brown habit that swept the ground. Her head and hair were completely covered so that only her face showed, a face lifted toward heaven, eyes closed, clearly praying. Believe it or not, I'd never seen a nun in full habit before—at least not in person. I couldn't help but think of the Reverend Mother in *The Sound of Music,* though this nun was clearly far younger, probably about forty.

"Her face looks so sweet," said one of our clinic workers. "But anguished."

There was an awkward silence. Then one of our clients, who had just had an abortion, was escorted out the door and to her car by one of volunteers. Our eyes were glued to the nun as, her eyes fixed on the client, she moved from the center of the driveway to the side, making room for the client to pull out of the drive. And then she began to weep. She fell to her knees and wept with such grief, such genuine personal pain, that I couldn't help but think to myself, *She feels something far deeper than I ever will. She is honestly pained. This is real to her—this grief at knowing that client had an abortion.* A sense of shame washed over me. I tried to shake it off but couldn't get past the fact that a nun was grieving over what was happening inside my clinic.

A silence fell over us all for a time. Several of our clinic staff were Catholic, but even those of us who weren't sensed a shared discomfort, as if we all felt embarrassed or ashamed. We tried to get back to work, but every few minutes someone would look out the window and offer an update on the sister, like, "She's still weeping," or, "Look, one of the pro-lifers is consoling her now." It was agony just knowing she was out there.

Over the next several months, we learned her name was Sister Marie Bernadette. She visited the fence, week after week, on abortion days. One of the clinic staff who often joked that she was a "recovering Catholic" complained one day at lunchtime. She had been planning to go out for lunch that day but said there was no way she was leaving the building because she didn't want the nun to see her.

The truth was, the sister's simple, prayerful presence bothered most of us, Catholic, ex-Catholic, Protestant, and unchurched alike, as if she somehow represented our consciences. The sister was small, bubbly, and joyful. She had a radiant smile, yet clearly over the months we could continue to see that she was deeply and personally grieved by abortions. *How many other people cry outside my workplace because of the work I am doing?* I wondered. I didn't like the question.

Over time we found ways to tease ourselves about the "power" of Sister Marie Bernadette as we came to realize we all avoided going outside when she was present. I found it eerie that her presence seemed to pervade the entire clinic every time she showed up at the fence.

Her simple presence always reminded me of confession.

CHAPTER TEN

The Hurricane

THIS PERIOD OF MY JOURNEY began with a hurricane—maybe that should have told me something.

From the fall of 2008 on, I faced increasing challenges both inside and outside my clinic, and my place within the movement for which I'd worked so hard was swept in a new direction seemingly overnight.

Everyone remembers Hurricane Katrina, which hit New Orleans and the Alabama Gulf coast with such force in 2005, and Hurricane Rita, which came shortly thereafter and devastated Houston. Except for those of us who lived through it, fewer remember Hurricane Ike, which hit the Caribbean and the Texas and Louisiana coast in September 2008, even though Ike was in fact the third costliest hurricane in U.S. history. It also killed forty-eight people in the United States; twenty-three others are still unaccounted for.

Fortunately those of us in the Bryan/College Station area were far enough inland to escape the worst of the storm, but we still experienced harsher weather than many people will see in a lifetime. It's not surprising, then, that as the hurricane approached, nearly everyone in the Planned Parenthood hierarchy expected we would close the clinic until the storm passed. As director of the clinic, I reported to Cheryl, who was now our regional director, and Cheryl, like everyone else, urged that we close the clinic.

I understood their reasons for wanting to close. We didn't yet know how bad the hurricane would get, even this far inland, and if we stayed open, our clients, staff, and visiting doctors risked injury from flooding, falling trees, and automobile accidents caused by dangerous road conditions and poor visibility—all the things that claim lives in any hurricane. But there was another concern, one that to my mind trumped the safety issue. We offered abortions only every other Saturday. If we closed the clinic, we would miss one of our abortion Saturdays, and those women who had been waiting would have to wait at least another two weeks. I was concerned that this delay could jeopardize their physical health since later abortions pose more risks. Not only that, from my own experience I knew how emotionally wrenching it would be to have to postpone the procedure.

Cheryl agreed it was unfortunate but said the clinic needed to be closed anyway.

At that point, I made it a personal campaign to keep the clinic open. Understand that at this point I had completely personalized my relationship with the clinic. I was the clinic, and the clinic was me. I took both our successes and our failures personally, and my self-respect was closely tied to how well the clinic performed. I got on the phone and talked to our staff and to the visiting doctors.

I may be stubborn, but I would not put my staff at risk. I knew that if the weather got bad enough, we simply wouldn't be able to stay open. And the worst of the storm was expected to hit on Saturday, September 13. Our affiliate leadership told me that I absolutely could not open the clinic that Saturday. So I arranged with the doctor to come in on Friday instead. Then my assistant and I called every patient scheduled to come in on Saturday and rescheduled their appointments for Friday. Every other Planned Parenthood clinic in the path of the hurricane was closed that Friday—except for us.

The weather was strange that day, as it often is when a hurricane is approaching. It was so still, gray, and eerie. It was hot, but every now and then the weather would turn oddly cool, and we'd say, "It's coming—we've got to move these women through here and get them home." But when we'd finished, the hurricane still hadn't hit. We had turned no one away, and everyone was able to head home with a reasonable expectation of arriving there.

And sure enough, on Saturday the weather was horrible—trees down across the roads, power out, flooding, high winds. There was no way we'd have been able to open on Saturday.

About a month later our statewide director made a statement celebrating the fact that even in the midst of a hurricane, our clinics had been open to provide services to women. Of course, only one had been open in the area affected by the storm—mine! You have to remember that when Hurricane Ike struck, I still fully embraced Planned Parenthood's pro-choice position. The organization—and what I saw as our shared mission to help women in crisis—had become of paramount concern to me. I was willing to risk anything to do what I thought was best for our clients.

A couple of months later, at our affiliate meeting in Houston, we had our first chance to get together and debrief about the hurricane and the resulting damage. We'd all seen plenty of destruction driving to the meeting that day, because Houston had been pretty well devastated by Ike. There had been serious flooding and lots of broken windows and damaged roofs. Power had been out in some areas of Houston for a full month after the hurricane, and grocery store shelves had been empty for weeks—not just because people immediately bought up anything the stores were able to stock, but also because they weren't able to get trucks in with food.

Our boardroom was on the first floor of a clinic in Houston—quite a large building, with administrative offices downstairs and a clinic upstairs. The boardroom was typical—lots of large tables set in a rectangle, with room for probably fifty. Barbara, the chief operating officer, had brought Christmas cookies. She and the other officers, senior VPs, and directors sat at the head, with the rest of us from the affiliate clinics filling up the rest of the rectangle. Our affiliate had twelve clinics: ten of them in Texas and the other two in Louisiana.

The meeting started with small talk, mostly about the hurricane—the devastation to so many homes, which areas had been damaged, which clinics had been hit, and so on. We snacked on Barbara's cookies as we chatted. Generally, our affiliate meetings didn't dwell to a large extent on financials, so we didn't expect that this one would. But partway through the meeting, Barbara announced that she had some really bad news for everybody. The projection screen had been pulled down from the ceiling, and now she raised it—revealing the whiteboard, on which she had already written a column of numbers. And believe me, the bottom line was not good.

Barbara's demeanor (despite the cookies) had been unsettled throughout the meeting, and by this point she looked not just stern but angry. Some of the bad news on the whiteboard was because of the costs associated with the hurricane, but some of it was due to not bringing in as much money as we were spending.

It was horrible news, of course. But most of the others felt as I did: *How is this our fault? We've had a hurricane, the economy is in crisis, and we've been working as hard as we can.* Some weeks I'd been spending nearly sixty hours on the job. If our finances were in bad shape, it wasn't from lack of trying.

Barbara referred us to the information packets we had been given, where we would find a list of the cost-cutting measures every clinic was to put into effect.

So we opened the packets and took a look. And were confused.

"Barbara," I said, "are these kinds of measures really going to make a difference?" Most of the emphasis was on conserving supplies—cutting down on the amount of cleaning supplies used, recycling envelopes, and conserving paper. Were we really so bad off?

She explained that it all came down to trying to get the affiliate's finances under control, and despite our best efforts, that hadn't been happening.

Even so, after that meeting, I was optimistic. Sure, the previous few months had been financially difficult. But we would put some of these cost-cutting measures into effect at all of our clinics, and hopefully by the next affiliate meeting the ugly numbers we'd seen would look a lot different. I really didn't think that our Bryan clinic was a problem—we were already following many of the cost-cutting measures Barbara had suggested anyway, and we started implementing the others. I figured that the other clinics just weren't being run as efficiently as ours. The Bryan clinic, I proudly believed, ran like a well-oiled machine.

Our next affiliate meeting was a few months later, and sure enough, the financial figures Barbara unveiled looked very different from the ones at the previous meeting—they were worse. The bottom line was truly ugly and truly scary.[7]

Barbara launched into an impassioned speech about how this couldn't continue, but after several minutes I interrupted her. "We're doing everything you've asked us to do," I said, frustrated. "If that's not enough, stop yelling at us and tell us what else we can do, because if we're going to turn this around, we need answers! And obviously that list of cost-cutting measures wasn't it!"

She was quiet for a moment, and then she said, "Well, we're wondering if we have too many people on staff."

There it was. The answer you always fear. Are we going to have to lay off some of our staff?

"I can't function with any fewer staff than I have now," I said, "not if we're to provide the same level of service. We're already shorthanded because I haven't been able to get permission to hire anyone."

Barbara said she planned to meet with each director individually. In the next couple of weeks, each of us would need to come to headquarters for a day. Barbara would evaluate each clinic with the director. They'd look at the clinic's schedule and discuss how to better schedule patients. They'd consider staff cuts if appropriate and necessary.

I feared their plan might be to increase the hours each of the staff would work, though they would be paid the same amount of money as before. Morale was already low. But it was about to get exponentially worse.

Or so I feared. But in a few days, when the scheduling of those meetings was to begin, Cheryl called with great news! The Bryan clinic was the only clinic that was meeting its goals. I was exempt from the meeting, she told me. "Congratulations."

I admit, I felt pretty good about that. I thought, *Yes! I must be doing something right.*

Actually, I had a few reasons to think that. For one, I'd just recently been named our affiliate's 2008 Employee of the Year. And besides that, Cheryl asked me to help her set up improved scheduling and procedures for the other clinics. So not only was my clinic not asked to make any changes, I was entrusted with developing a plan to guide other clinics to greater financial health.

There's one thing none of us mentioned, though. It was easier for my clinic to meet its goals and stay on sound financial footing compared to most others. We were one of the few clinics in our affiliate that performed abortions. And those abortions earned a lot of money. The clinics that didn't perform abortions had little means of providing revenue.

Things got worse for our affiliate as the year progressed. We were moving further and further into the red, and by mid-spring of 2009 we were forced to lay people off. At first no one from my clinic was terminated—although good friends from other clinics were being let go—but then my clinic lost one part-timer.

The month after that second affiliate meeting, I was braced for more bad news, but nothing compared to what I received. And this time, it had nothing to do with the budget. Or did it?

Planned Parenthood, we learned, was planning to open a massive seven-story, 78,000-square-foot clinic in Houston, and supposedly an entire floor was being devoted to medical and abortion services. I understood that it could be the largest abortion clinic in the nation, and that plans were in place to seek an ambulatory surgical license, which would qualify the facility to perform late-term abortions, possibly up to twenty-four weeks.[8]

My stomach knotted at the news. I'd always believed that

late-term abortions beyond the age of viability (twenty-one to twenty-four weeks) were wrong. I'd always insisted I would never work for an organization that performed late-term abortions.

I can't do it. I won't do it. I've always said I'd draw the line there. But rumors were flying, as any Google search will show you. They'd start the clinic going to sixteen weeks as their current license permitted. But I got conflicting reports, internally, depending on who I spoke to, about the actual plans for late-term abortions. I heard they'd never go beyond sixteen weeks, I heard nineteen weeks, and I heard twenty-four weeks. This was my affiliate. Why would they go that high? This wasn't about access to care. I knew that. The percentage of late-term abortions is fairly low, and there was already a Houston abortion clinic (not part of Planned Parenthood) that performed that ghastly procedure.

Why was our leadership supposedly planning to get into the business? Wasn't our stated goal to *decrease* the number of abortions? Hadn't that talking point been drummed into me from the day I was recruited, to Lobby Day, to my media training? Didn't I teach this to my own staff? There was nothing preventative about aborting viable babies. What greater good would be served? I didn't like any of the answers that came to me.

I could only conjecture, of course, but in light of the budget discussions, I couldn't help but do the math. The later the abortion, the higher the cost. A late-term abortion, I knew, could cost between $3,000 and $4,000. There was big money to be made. Could this be driving Planned Parenthood?

The question haunted me.

CHAPTER ELEVEN

The Boardroom

In May, there was even more bad news.

We entered the boardroom for our management meeting of clinic directors only to learn that our Title XX money had run out. Title XX is a section of the United States Code that provides funds for social services. Planned Parenthood was one of many recipients, since we provided birth control and family planning. Now that money was gone.[9]

Our affiliate meeting that month was a bloodbath. I was told we were no longer going to offer birth control pills at a discounted rate to lower-income women. I asked why, though I feared I already knew the answer. The spreadsheets. The big red number.

"What?" I said. "So because we're in debt, we suddenly don't care if lower-income women get pregnant with babies they can't afford to have or raise? We are just going to cut off these women on our birth control plan overnight?" And the conversation went downhill from there. Many people were angry and expressed their frustration that administrators at headquarters seemed to be more concerned about the bottom line than our clients.

Sure, I know that was unfair—you can't spend money you don't have. But financial woes or not, we saw ourselves as those who cared about the plight of women in crisis. At least, that's how some of us saw ourselves.

"But we are nonprofit!" I declared in a passionate plea.

"Abby," I was told pointedly, "nonprofit is a tax status, not a business status." I was ordered to get my priorities straight—which meant I had to get my revenue up. As the meeting continued, I sat there stunned.

Get my revenue up? Since when has generating revenue been our goal? I couldn't believe what I was hearing.

Each year, each clinic has an individual budget meeting. With a feeling of dread I drove to Houston to meet with Cheryl and Barbara to receive the budget for my clinic. The assigned budget always includes a line for client goals under abortion services and a line for client goals under family planning.

When I looked at the numbers, I did a double take. I noticed that the client goals related to family planning hadn't changed much, but the client goals under abortion services had increased significantly. My mind started racing. *Something's got to be wrong here. Shouldn't it be the other way around? Our goal at Planned Parenthood is to decrease the number of abortions by decreasing the number of unwanted pregnancies. That means family planning services—birth control. That is our stated goal. So why am I being asked, according to this budget, to increase my abortion revenue and thus my abortion client count?*

And so I asked the question out loud.

I came away from that meeting with the clear and distinct understanding that I was to get my priorities straight, that abortion was where my priorities needed to be because that was where the revenue was. This meant that my job as the clinic director was to find a way to increase the number of abortions at my clinic.[10]

To say the least, I was appalled.

"Abortion will *never* be my priority!" I insisted. "Never."

The discussion continued for some time. Let's just say it was pretty bumpy.

What had happened to my world? Following the instructions of my employer, rather than limit all abortions to every other Saturday, we now expanded medication abortions to every day of the week. If someone called for an abortion, they could have it the next day if they wanted to use RU-486 instead of surgical abortion. How easy and convenient that sounded to many clients, and sure enough, our abortion numbers started going up.

But this wasn't what I'd signed up for.

Even so, I wasn't ready to walk away from the career I'd been building. I loved serving women. I enjoyed my staff. Megan and Taylor had become dear friends by now, and the culture of compassion we all shared in the work we did—the good work of helping women—was a bond I treasured. I didn't want to just walk away. I wanted to fight for the right to run my clinic according to what I'd always been told and always believed were our true purposes. Surely I could work to persuade my affiliate to honor its true mission, couldn't I? I convinced myself that was my goal, and so I stayed.

As if May had not been bad enough, the last day of the month dealt a terrible blow to all of us at the clinic. Doug, Grace, and I were having lunch at a restaurant after church when my cell phone rang. It was Cheryl, with horrible news. Dr. George Tiller, the abortionist from Wichita, had been gunned down by an antiabortion extremist while attending his church that morning.

I was speechless when she told me. I barely managed to get the words out to tell Doug. I couldn't eat anymore. Doug was terrified for my safety. I went out to the car with Grace, he boxed up our food, and then we immediately went home. A few minutes later, we saw it as breaking news on CNN. I remember feeling so exposed, like everyone suddenly knew I worked in the abortion industry . . . and maybe I was next. That first day was terrifying. Doug wouldn't let me leave the house. He was scared. My extended family was scared. I was trying to downplay it . . . but unsuccessfully. I called all of my employees to let them know and to touch base with them and see how they were doing.

But the next morning my shock gave way to anger. When I went into work on Monday, I felt like I was going into battle—battle against the pro-lifers for my staff. I didn't really feel that it was about me; it was about them and our clients. As I drove past a couple of people praying at the fence, I thought, *How dare they show up today.* I considered it disrespectful of them to be there on a day when all of us on staff were scared and grieving.

I had already received death threats . . . and now this. For weeks, every day when I went to work I would replay in my mind the escape strategy for my employees if someone were to come in wielding a gun or a bomb. I figured they would want me, the director. So every day as I drove in, I'd think through which employees were working that day, where their offices were, how I could get their attention to get them out of the building, etc. My goal would be to get them out and to leave me in. It was a stressful thought, but one that I constantly thought of. And it was a responsibility I was willing to accept. I figured that when I took on the job as director, my ultimate responsibility was to keep my staff safe . . . at any cost, even if it was my life. Dr. Tiller's murder had given our work and our bond a new and deeper meaning. I truly felt like an officer in wartime who needed to protect my troops.

And my troops were scared. In the wake of the previous death threats I had assured them that they had been threats, nothing more. But now someone we knew and admired had been gunned down. The Web sites went wild with chatter, and the responses of pro-lifers to the murder just fueled our anger, no matter how they responded. We found it unconscionable that some celebrated his murder as a victory for the pro-life cause. How could a murder benefit a cause that stood for life? But it also made us angry that so many pro-life groups were coming out with statements condemning the murderer's actions. It seemed to be false sympathy for the victim. The relationships at the fence cooled as well. Everyone was guarded and tense.

Dr. Tiller's death so solidified our cause, so rallied our sense of being the despised yet brave advocates for women's health and well-being, that my concerns about budgets and abortion goals faded to the background. I was no victim, and Planned Parenthood was no ill-willed organization, I told myself. I was a warrior in a noble battle. I do realize how melodramatic that sounds, but such was the impact of the murder of one of the pioneers in our realm of women's reproductive rights.

It was in August 2009, only about a month before my experience with the fateful ultrasound-guided abortion, that the receptionist at the clinic referred a call to me. "I think you'll want to take this one."

"Do you have a back parking area at the clinic?" the caller asked. "One where I can't be seen from the road?"

"I'm afraid not," I said. "All of our parking is in the front. Is there a problem?" It hadn't yet been three full months since Dr. Tiller's death, and security was still a major concern to us.

The young woman hesitated. "No, it's not that big of a deal," she said. "It's just that my family is outside the clinic praying." Well, yes, that could be a problem. "They know I'm having an abortion today," she added. "They're trying to talk me out of it."

"How about this," I suggested. "You park as close to the building as you can. We'll come out and escort you in. But you should understand that you will be visible from the fence."

Cheryl was at the clinic that day, since she always came in on the days we provided surgical abortions. She and I watched for the woman from the window. And naturally, the client did *not* park close to the building—she parked right next to the fence. I could see her family group outside the fence—there were several of them. One woman, who seemed particularly upset, seemed the right age to be her mother.

Usually I was busy with administrative work inside and let our volunteers go out to escort the women in. But this time I told Cheryl, "I'm going out there."

Cheryl suggested I bring her in the back entrance. She'd bring the paperwork there so the client wouldn't have to go through the waiting room at all. I thought that was a good idea, figuring the young woman would be a basket case by then.

As I approached the girl's car, she got out on one side and the friend who had accompanied her got out on the other. Her mom was standing just outside the fence calling to her, obviously in real emotional pain. The rest of the family stood in a semicircle behind the mom. I stepped up beside the girl and put my hand on her back. "I'll bring you around to the back entrance. It'll be quicker that way."

The girl didn't answer. The mother's voice, through her weeping, was filled with desperation. "You don't have to do this," she called, her voice anguished. "We want to help you. We can support you. You can live at home. We'll give you money—whatever it takes! Don't do this." Her mother's pleas were so heartbreaking that my heart was pounding with the tension.

And as I stood waiting, the back door of the car opened and a little girl got out—maybe two years old. It was the daughter of the girl who'd come in to have the abortion! And as she stepped up beside her mother, she saw her grandmother on the other side of the fence. "Hey, Mamá!" she called innocently.

The grandmother wept even harder. Hanging on to the fence now as if to support herself, she cried out, "The baby you're carrying will be just as beautiful as the daughter you already have! Just think if you had decided to abort her—think of all the joy she has brought into our lives. Imagine a world without her! Please—you don't have to do this!"

It was the most intense moment I've ever witnessed between a mother and daughter. Clearly, here was a woman who felt that her child was about to make one of the biggest decisions of her life—and was making the *wrong* decision. One this mother clearly believed her daughter would regret the rest of her life.

I was so conscious at that moment of the meaning of the fence, both physical and symbolic. It was a physical barrier between that young woman and the mother who so clearly wanted to scale the fence and take her daughter into her arms. And it was a symbolic barrier, too—symbolic of the divide between the mother who valued the life of this unborn child so much she pled for it, begged for it, wept for it; and the daughter who didn't see what the big deal was.

And she didn't. I escorted her inside. "Are you all right? Do you need to talk about this first? Are you sure this is what you want to do? Because it sounds like you'd have a lot of support from your family if you were to keep the baby."

I am not sure what I expected, but it wasn't what I saw next. She shrugged it off. "Oh, that's just my mom," she said. "That's how she is. I'm fine."

Fine? How could she be *fine*? If that had been my mother I'd have been a wreck! As a matter of fact, I *was* a wreck. I was deeply shaken by her mother's pleas. They had pierced my armor. I stepped back, somewhat stunned. I turned and went back to my office, sat at my desk, and began to weep. I couldn't have told you, at the time, why I was weeping. I'd have said maybe it was because of the emotional intensity of it all. Or maybe because of the rift between mother and daughter. But from some deep well within me, the tears came.

Maybe, just maybe, that secret box hidden deep within me, nailed shut so that my two abortions couldn't speak to me, was crying out that my babies hadn't had anyone pleading for their lives when I stepped into a clinic to abort them. Of course, I'd never told my mom and dad I was pregnant. But if I had and they had met me at the abortion clinic to offer to help me through my crisis pregnancies, would I have gone through with those abortions?

I checked the window occasionally to see what the family would do. They continued to stand and pray for an hour, then another hour. Then finally they left.

The young woman had her abortion, spent her time recovering, and three or four hours after she arrived, she took her daughter and her friend and left. I never saw her again. But I never forgot her mother's anguished pleading for the life of her grandchild through the fence.

The scales were beginning to fall from my eyes. This family's attempt to save the life of the baby they were ready to love and care for woke me from the haze of Dr. Tiller's murder and brought to the surface my discovery of Planned Parenthood's revenue agenda. I'd always believed everything Planned Parenthood told me—that our purpose was to fight for and provide for the reproductive and health rights of women, that the organization had been born out of a desire to help women in crisis. But when the bottom dropped out, financially speaking, it suddenly seemed to me that the organization was getting off track.

I was starting to put the pieces together. I couldn't escape the thought that this organization that had given me my career would soon be in the late-term abortion business. My dilemma was deep and profound. I was finding it increasingly hard to justify what I now saw as Planned Parenthood's money-first attitude toward abortion, especially late-term abortions. I felt I was being forced into a decision. And as yet, I wasn't sure what the criteria for that decision needed to be.

Here is the point in my journey where you already know what happened next. I opened this book with my turning point. I can only assume, given all that had led to this moment, that I needed God's intervention in a huge way to make a complete break with the organization that had once meant so much to me. And God provided that intervention. He had me beckoned into the exam room that September day in 2009. He had me witness the ultrasound-guided abortion with my own eyes.

CHAPTER TWELVE

A Holy Hush

God is a great choreographer, isn't He? As I take a hard look now at the fateful day of the ultrasound-guided abortion—that horrible, crushing, startling, eye-opening day—I see how perfectly He had positioned me so that when my eyes were pried open by His fingers, I'd have the clearest possible view. And I don't just mean the view of that precious unborn child violently sacrificed on the table that day. I mean the view of the Planned Parenthood trap into which I'd fallen.

You have now witnessed my journey from the Flag Room to the abortion room. You now understand that I saw the ultrasound-guided abortion within days of being mandated to increase the abortion revenue at my clinic, and this from the organization that had recruited me by telling me they wanted to make abortion rare.

Now that the scales had begun to fall from my eyes, the guilt of countless abortions, including my own two, came crashing down on my shoulders.

I walked slowly back to my office after checking on the patient for at least the fourth time. I'd made sure she was comfortable and warm enough, but I'd avoided making eye contact. Images of the abortion I'd just witnessed on the ultrasound monitor continued to play through my mind, and I felt eerily unfocused and dazed, almost as if I were caught in slow motion. There was no going back. No undoing what I'd just participated in.

I closed my office door behind me, something I rarely did. Then I lowered myself into my chair and just sat there, not really focusing on anything. Just staring. I wasn't crying. I simply felt the enormity of the moment. I found it hard to get a deep breath. I'd just participated in a death. A *death*. Not a medical procedure. Not a surgical solution to a life problem. Not the valiant step of a woman exercising her right to make medical choices about her own body. The death of a helpless baby, a baby violently ripped away from the safety of the womb, sucked away to be discarded as biohazard waste.

Beam me up, Scotty. The abortionist's lighthearted quip echoed in my head.

And I was just as culpable as he. I'd scheduled countless babies for their deaths. I'd presented confused, anxious, and panicked women with their options—parent, abort, or adopt—as if we were discussing menu options. And when they chose to abort, I'd laid out their options again—surgical or medication—with their safety and comfort in mind, and all the while a tiny baby, tucked securely inside a womb, had been in the same room with us, with no one to speak on his or her behalf.

I can't do this anymore. I've made my decision. I'll never be part of another abortion in any way. I'm giving up my career. That's it—I'm out of here. It hit me then, so clearly that I found myself shaking my head to somehow sort out the new thoughts suddenly flying at me from every direction. *This has been a long time coming. Everything that's been happening for months has led me to this moment. How could I have missed seeing this for what it is?*

Suddenly, I became aware of the time. How long had I been sitting here? Probably only about ten or fifteen minutes. A sudden fear shot through me—not an emotion I'm used to. What if the doctor called me back to help with the next abortion? *I am not going back in that room. They can find someone else. I need to get busy, fast.* So I stood, took a deep breath to gather my composure, opened my office door, and headed to the front desk to help with the billing. The sooner we got the billing done, the sooner we'd all get out of there. And I wanted out of there badly. With my head down and hands busy, no one interrupted me. The rest of the workday was a blur, but before long the place was closed up.

Driving home, I tried to imagine how I'd tell Doug. *What will I say? Where will I begin?*

Doug was in the living room when I got home. "Hey, babe. How was your day?" he asked.

"I've got to tell you what I saw today," I blurted, "but you're not gonna want to hear it. I mean, it's horrible—but I've got to describe it. I've got to tell somebody." My words tumbled out so fast I couldn't stop them.

He stood up, his alarm and concern clear. "What is it, Abby? What's wrong?"

And I told him. I described every detail of the abortion I had witnessed. And I watched his face twist in disgust.

"You're right. I don't want to hear this," he said, looking pained, stricken.

"I know," I nearly shouted, "but I can't get this out of my head. It keeps replaying over and over. That tiny little spine just crumpling into the tube, right before my eyes. Doug, if everyone who works there saw what I saw today, half of them would quit in an instant. I know it. They wouldn't still be there. Eight years I've been there, and until today I never truly saw what we do. How could I have been so stupid, so blind?"

"I know," he whispered. "I know." We were sitting on the couch now, his left arm around my shoulders, his right hand caressing my own hands as I twisted them in my lap, these hands that had helped deprive a child of life. We sat until I could sit still no longer. I jumped up.

"I've got to call Valerie. I've got to tell her." I dialed my closest friend's number and described the entire scene again, as if by telling it aloud I could stop it playing in my mind.

"I can't listen to this," Valerie finally said. "Don't talk about it. Please stop." I understood, of course. If only I could make it stop in my mind.

Doug and I talked long into the night.

"What are we going to do?" I asked, not really expecting an answer. "Eight years of my life I've given to this cause. I don't want to walk away. We do so much good at the clinic. How many lives do we save? Lots, I'm sure. All the community education I've done on STDs and protected sex. The testing, the Pap smears, the adoptions. And what if we hadn't done those abortions? Do you know the lives some of those babies would be living? Abuse. Neglect. The never-ending cycle of poverty. I mean, I know what I saw today was horrible, was wrong. But choice still has to be right, doesn't it? Lots of those women are desperate, Doug. If they can't get a safe abortion from us, they are just going to get butchered. Isn't it better to have an ugly but safe abortion than an ugly but dangerous one?"

The more I talked, the more confused I got. One thing I was sure of: I sure wasn't "switching sides" to join those pro-lifers.

Was I?

No. I wasn't. I couldn't have been wrong about that for these last eight years. Whether I liked abortion or not, women still needed the right to make that decision for themselves and they still needed safe clinics where they could go to have the procedure done. And here in Texas they didn't have many such places.

"I'm not switching sides, you know," I told Doug. "But I'm not going to ever be part of an abortion again. I know it's wrong. I see that now. It's wrong for me, and it's ugly. But I'm not joining up with people who think they have a right to impose their views on people who don't agree with them. Those Coalition people are still wrong. It's not right to impose one's view on other people. I am still pro-choice. But I, personally, am through with taking part in abortion."

"So what you saw today, Abby, is okay as long as you are not personally involved?"

"No! It's not okay. But . . . I . . . I think I've handled all I can for one day! I'm done."

We were in agreement that I would leave Planned Parenthood. Beyond that, who knew?

We also agreed that I needed to find another job fast.

"Okay. So I've got two weeks to find a new job then," I said as we wrapped up the conversation, both exhausted. "Two weeks. Because I will not be present for another Saturday abortion day, and the next one is two weeks from today."

I can see now something I couldn't see then: pride. I was worried. Worried that maybe I'd been wrong for eight years. Worried that I'd been fighting on the wrong side of the battle. I was afraid that night even to imagine how humiliating and embarrassing it would be to have to go public with the acknowledgment that I'd been wrong. After all, I hadn't been a *private* advocate of choice; I'd been a highly vocal, public champion of choice. At that point I couldn't imagine I'd been wrong on the importance of women having access to legal, safe abortions, even if I now despised the act of abortion.

Something else strikes me as I look back on that night. I am intensely aware that my kind husband never once said, "I tried to tell you." Despite all the debates and arguments we'd had, despite all the times he'd challenged my faulty thinking and I'd refused to hear the truth—there he sat, comforting and loving me. What a picture of Ephesians 5:25: "Husbands, love your wives, just as Christ loved the church." His compassion and support were the beginning of my healing that day. But I still had a long way to go.

The next day was Sunday. When I woke up, my right hand, the hand that had held the ultrasound probe the day before, was aching. I examined it and massaged it, and though I could find nothing obviously wrong, it was terribly sore. As I dressed and fixed my hair, it hurt so badly that I found it hard to hold anything. In my shock while watching the ultrasound-guided abortion, had I unknowingly gripped the probe too tightly? I don't know. But all the way to church it hurt.

As Doug and I took our seats, we said hello to Megan, who sat directly in front of us. What would I say to her tomorrow at work? I didn't have a clue, but I couldn't bring it up to her here. Not today. I'd lose it, make a scene, and do more harm than good. My emotions were too raw.

When the service began, I took comfort in the familiar words of the liturgy, which had been haunting me in recent months.

> Almighty God, to you all hearts are open, all desires known, and from you no secrets are hid. Cleanse the thoughts of our hearts by the inspiration of your Holy Spirit, that we may perfectly love you and worthily magnify your Name, through Christ our Lord.[11]

Well, the secrets have never been hidden from You, God, and now they aren't hidden from me anymore either. I've seen them. I repent. I turn away. Never again, never again, Lord.

The words of the liturgy were leaping from the page with power.

> Create in me a clean heart, O God, and renew a right spirit within me.[12]

Never in my life had words of confession spilled out of me with such fervor. And as they spilled out, I sensed God's love and forgiveness pouring in. Yet my hand kept hurting.

As the pastor began reading the Gospel lesson for the day, I couldn't believe my ears. He read from Mark 9:43: "If your hand causes you to sin, cut it off. It is better for you to enter life maimed than with two hands to go into hell, where the fire never goes out."

A holy hush fell over my soul. *If your hand causes you to sin . . .* God was speaking directly to me this morning. My hand hurt even as I heard those words!

None of this was coincidence. None of it was chance. It was confirmed to me in that moment that God had been working a long time to break through to me. He'd spoken through my husband, but I'd argued his voice away. He'd spoken through the peaceful and gentle ways of those who prayed at the fence, through flowers and a card from Elizabeth two years before (she had since moved to Austin), through Mr. Orozco's warmth and joy and steadfast presence every Wednesday and Saturday morning of the year, through Bobby's befriending every new Planned Parenthood volunteer, through a weeping nun. But I'd brushed off the whole Coalition for Life crowd as naive zealots with their heads buried in the sand.

God had spoken through my mother's honest, firm, yet loving words, but I'd avoided and discounted them as old-fashioned and out of touch. He'd spoken through the agonized, pleading cries of the client's mother I remembered, pleading for the life of her grandchild through the fence as her daughter entered our clinic to abort that child, but I had missed the message.

He'd even exposed Planned Parenthood's motives and intentions to me as plain as day through their own words and mandates, and though I'd fumed and protested and complained and fought against them, I'd still not seen the truth. Maybe my coworkers and I were there to help women in crisis, but I no longer saw Planned Parenthood as a benevolent charitable organization with the goal of decreasing unwanted pregnancies. I was now convinced that it was an abortion machine in the business of killing unborn babies and meeting revenue goals. And my hands, my words, my energy, and my passion—all had been tools of this machine.

My eyes landed on Megan, directly in front of me. I hoped she was listening to that verse the same way that I was, but somehow I knew she wasn't. I began praying for her, that God would speak to her in the same way.

Our hands are causing us to sin.

Our mouths are causing us to sin.

Open her eyes. Open her ears.

As Doug and I exited at the end of the service, I whispered to him about my hand and the verse. His eyes opened wide; we shared a moment of awe that God was communicating clearly and directly with me that morning. When we got home, I didn't waste a minute. I jumped online and began filling out job applications, checking out job Web sites. I was determined to find a new job within two weeks and be out of Planned Parenthood before we performed surgical abortions again.

But I only had a few hours to devote to my hunt. Months before I'd committed to a KEOS radio interview with the host of the program *Fair and Feminist*. It was a program very sympathetic to Planned Parenthood, and I'd been a guest on the show before. We'd planned this one knowing that the 40 Days for Life campaign would be in full swing—the perfect opportunity to attract new supporters to the pro-choice cause.

"Doug, you know I've got that radio interview tonight."

"Oh, I'd forgotten all about it. What are you going to do?"

"Well, I don't see I've got much of a choice. I'm committed. But I don't have to talk about my personal feelings on abortion. I can just stick to the talking points, like I always do. I'm still representing Planned Parenthood. I'll follow my usual script and get it over with."

That is just what I did. The program's host was a friend, a volunteer at the clinic even. She and I had shared our dislike for the Coalition for Life's views, and frankly, I still disliked them. It was the oddest sensation to do the interview that night. On the one hand, it was surprisingly simple to slip into the role of media spokesperson and use the well-rehearsed words I'd said a thousand times. But on the other hand, this time I felt that I was acting a role rather than speaking my heart. It wasn't a feeling I liked, not one bit. I came away from the interview feeling a bit sick to my stomach. I really wanted to believe I could personally hate abortion and yet be a proponent of choice. Lots of people in my own church held that view, I knew.

But now it made me squirm. It had to be the right view, didn't it? Then why didn't this ring true?

And what of the holy hush I'd felt in church just that morning? It all seemed so black-and-white that morning. Now the gray was floating in.

CHAPTER THIRTEEN

Inside Out

I hope I won't be coming through this gate too many more times, I thought. And so began my first morning at the clinic since the ultrasound-guided abortion. Funny. For eight years I'd been pulling up this drive and though this gate, and each time I'd been certain that the fence was keeping "the enemy" out. Today, for the very first time, I wondered if my thinking had been inside out.

Outside the fence, Bobby, one of the regular Coalition for Life volunteer trainers, was already talking to some new sidewalk recruit. They were six days into their fall 40 Days for Life campaign, so during every hour of every twenty-four-hour day at least two people were praying, standing, kneeling, or strolling along the fence. Lots of them were familiar faces, like Bobby. But there were newcomers, too. I wondered what he was telling the new gal. And how did they recruit so many new volunteers every year? I'd just slammed these people on the radio the night before. Did negative publicity like that diminish their numbers or strengthen them?

As I pulled up the drive and parked, I was thinking that a lot had changed since my first days as a Planned Parenthood volunteer back in 2001. I thought about the Grim Reaper in full costume and the woman with the awful placard with the photo of the aborted fetus. It had been years since we'd seen their brand of protesting here at the Bryan clinic, thanks largely to the peaceful, respectful presence of the Coalition for Life. I'd thought of those two in particular as crazies. Now I wondered about their stories. What had driven them to such measures? What had they seen that had stirred them to such action? Whom had they lost? It was the first time these questions had ever occurred to me.

And I didn't like the questions one bit. Good intentions or not, these zealots had to be wrong. Okay, sure; abortion is ugly. Now I'd finally seen that for myself. But life is ugly; ugly things happen. Women need access to safety and health care when they find themselves with an unwanted pregnancy, right? Right? I was asking myself the question, but was no longer sure of the answer. After years of fighting for this cause, I didn't like the feeling that maybe I was wrong.

And if I was wrong, did that mean these pro-lifers were right? No. I couldn't go there. I'd been fighting them too long. They had to be wrong.

To my relief, it was a quiet day at the clinic. I kept my head down and did my best to avoid conversation that day, and the next, and Wednesday and Thursday, too. I stayed focused on the administrative tasks at hand, avoided the clients, and just kept to myself. At least in person. E-mail was another story. Cheryl and I were exchanging a barrage of frustrating e-mails. Was it my imagination, or was she trying to micromanage my clinic? Ever since I'd challenged the mandates at the management meeting in Houston a few months ago, it seemed the tension between us had been growing. Now it appeared to be mounting exponentially.

I admit, I'm not much of a follower. Never have been. I like to lead. I speak my mind in a hurry and never hesitate to express disagreement. But that was nothing new to my boss, Cheryl. I'd worked with her since my start at Planned Parenthood, and we'd never had problems like this before. Why now?

Maybe the reason was that never before had we faced such a clear gap—no, more like a chasm, a gulf—over the very core, the values, the identity of Planned Parenthood. I'd been recruited to join an organization dedicated to helping women in crisis. I had always understood it to be charitable in nature, with the clear goal of decreasing the number of unwanted pregnancies and the number of abortions, to be a champion for struggling women, to put women's needs first and finances second. I'd successfully run the clinic that way since 2007, and for that I'd won Employee of the Year. Now with finances tight, I felt I was being forced to redefine who we were, and I thought it was my place, my duty, to fight for our true identity. But so far, the harder I pushed, the more upset Cheryl seemed to get.

"This is a business, Abby. Get your priorities straight."[13] That was the clear message I'd picked up in Houston. And this week in particular I felt I was being pushed harder and harder to make changes I deemed detrimental to our clients. Was that just my imagination? Or had seeing the ultrasound-guided abortion changed my interpretation of the messages? My self-doubt and inner confusion were growing. And frankly, my sense of no longer being valued as a star employee was chafing.

Meanwhile, my job hunt seemed stalled out. I hadn't received as much as a nibble on my online efforts at job hunting, and I couldn't make calls during the workday. The sense of mounting pressure, of wanting out, of despising the place, of feeling trapped was growing, and by Friday morning it was haunting me.

Anxious to accomplish something toward ending my involvement at the clinic, I began sorting through my desk and files, removing personal items. I found my stash of greeting cards from Boss's Day and special occasions, a few other odds and ends, and even my Employee of the Year award, and I stuffed them into a bag to take home. I didn't want to be obvious in any way, so I left my wall pictures and desktop photos and keepsakes in place.

I felt sneaky—not a pleasant feeling. But I also knew I couldn't let my colleagues know what was up yet. Given the tensions over the past few months, I knew there would be a scene, an uproar, if I told them I was job hunting—and I strongly suspected it would get back to Cheryl, and I was afraid she would find an unjust reason to fire me on the spot. Doug and I depended on my income, and I wanted to be able to seek out new employment on my own terms, as an employee in good standing. Besides, I had not yet been able to come up with the language for a rationale as to why I was leaving. How could I explain my change of heart without sounding like the very people I had always mocked—like some judgmental pro-life zealot, like the enemy on the other side of the fence?

I looked out my office window. There they were. The enemy. Three of them at the moment. Two middle-aged women and one twentysomething guy. Walking the fence. Praying. Speaking words of kindness to a client—a potential victim of Planned Parenthood—just parking her car to come into the facility. I knew their lines so well, having heard them now for years; I could repeat them in my sleep. Some enemy. Some weapons.

I squirmed at the memory of mocking them during Sunday's radio interview; of accusing them of harassing our clients; of my snide comments over the years, meant to intimidate their fresh recruits. It had been a very long time since I'd witnessed anyone on the other side of the fence say something that could really be called harassment, and I'd always known those tactics weren't approved by Shawn Carney and the Coalition for Life. I knew for a fact how hard he and his volunteers worked to train their "stand and pray" volunteers to be respectful, gentle, and pleasant. I'd watched them correct those who didn't show those qualities and diffuse tensions at the fence.

But our Planned Parenthood media talking points lumped all pro-lifers together rather than acknowledging that the movement is composed of many different individuals with very distinct goals and methods. Anything we could do to vilify the entire movement and paint ourselves as the victims of these antiabortion zealots accomplished our goals—it won donations and support, brought in fresh volunteers, and kept up the them-against-us, war-zone mentality.[14] Those were our goals. I'd been good at promoting them.

Victims. Now I was so confused about who the victims really were. Had I been a victim back when I'd been recruited at the volunteer fair? Fresh meat for the volunteer staff? Were my staff and I victims, thinking we were helping women while working so hard on behalf of our clients, when our efforts seemed to be used only to move budget numbers from red columns to black?

Another patient pulled up and parked. She hesitated before getting out of her car. Was she pregnant? If so, there were two new victims in that car. It was an ugly thought.

Everything seemed inside out.

And then the phone rang.

"Abby, this is Susan from HR in Houston. Could you come to Houston today? Cheryl and I would like to meet with you."

"Today? You need me to drive to Houston today? Why?" I couldn't imagine what this was about, but there was something odd about Susan's voice. An undercurrent of formality, of tension. I felt a wave of uneasiness. Were they on to me? Did they know I was planning to leave? How could they? Had one of my online applications been brought to their attention?

But Susan wouldn't tell. She simply insisted I drive to Houston. I hung up and called Doug right away. As I told him what Susan had said, I found myself getting more and more worked up.

"Are they going to fire me? If so, I have no idea what for."

"Fire you? Abby, how could they fire you? You just got the Employee of the Year award, for goodness' sake. You ace all the inspections. You're a star employee. How many times has Cheryl told you, 'One day my job will be yours, Abby'? They're not going to fire you. You're being paranoid. Just go to the meeting—you'll see."

The drive to Houston took about ninety minutes, but it felt like hours. I kept replaying recent management meetings over and over in my head. I had been very outspoken. I had protested the new cost-cutting measures, the increased costs to our clients, and especially the mandate to increase abortions. But surely speaking my mind at a meeting wasn't grounds for dismissal, was it? By the time I got to the Houston office I was both scared and angry, but I was ready to hear it. I wanted the truth out on the table.

"Abby," Susan explained, "we've called you here to let you know that you are being formally reprimanded. A reprimand is being placed in your employee file."

I couldn't believe what I was hearing.

"And what is it I'm being reprimanded for?" I looked straight at Cheryl, not at Susan. I wanted to hear it from her. And she spoke right up. She told me I'd been directly challenging her and her authority. I had become combative, disputing her directives, arguing and pushing back instead of doing what I was told.

I was dumbfounded. I'd always spoken my mind. I asked her if asking questions and pushing back on new policies was no longer allowed. Was I being told I wasn't permitted to ask questions or disagree?

She told me it was my place to do what I was told, just as it was her place to do what she was told. She was my supervisor, and it was my job to follow her instructions.

In my eight years with Planned Parenthood, I'd never received anything but praise. Never a single black mark, never a warning. I'd never received so much as a correction, much less a reprimand. My evaluations were great. It had been only a few months since they'd honored me publicly as Employee of the Year. I had a stellar record, and all three of us in that room knew it.

But it was what it was. Over the next hour or so, Susan led us through a discussion supposedly intended to resolve our differences. Finally she summed it up by pointing out that both Cheryl and I had very strong personalities. Susan said she hoped that, now that we'd had this talk, we could put this behind us. She concluded, "Abby, I need you to sign this acknowledgment that we've had this talk and informed you of the reprimand."

What could I do? I signed the paper. Cheryl looked smug and satisfied. I felt like a whipped dog—and, I confess, a resentful one. Cheryl had won. As I drove home, I kept wondering how a model employee whose performance was exceptional and whose clinic was known for excellence could have fallen from grace so quickly.

Doug had an interesting take on it that night as I debriefed with him: "Maybe God is telling you, plain and simple, that this is not where you should be."

I had to admit, that made more sense to me than any other explanation. I'd loved this job with a passion. I really didn't want to leave it, and I'd been struggling over that all week. The timing of all these factors—the mandate to increase abortions, my participation in the ultrasound-guided abortion, and now the reprimand—had to be more than coincidence. If God were going to choreograph my dance out of Planned Parenthood, He'd certainly chosen all the right moves. I just wished He'd show me the next step.

CHAPTER FOURTEEN

The Wrong Side of the Fence

IT HAD NOW BEEN ONE FULL WEEK since my participation in the ultrasound-guided abortion. My weekend would be devoted to job hunting, spurred on all the more by yesterday's reprimand. But that job hunt was hampered by my reluctance to call around to friends and associates. I didn't want word to get back to Planned Parenthood. I filled out more online applications and scouted medical and counseling clinics, but by Sunday night I was feeling pretty defeated. My anxiety was growing. One week left. My last day at the clinic would be Friday the ninth, job or no job. Doug and I needed to take a hard look at our finances and brace ourselves for a major loss of income.

I crawled into bed Sunday night feeling like a failure. Guilt was infiltrating my every thought. My sense of God's forgiveness from the previous Sunday morning had faded. God had no obligation to rescue me from my dilemma, I reasoned. I'd brought this all on myself, and I deserved to suffer for my sins. From my first days at Planned Parenthood, I'd told myself I was there to *decrease* the number of abortions.

Now, the absurdity of that logic—or lack of logic—screamed at me. Not only had I been a leader in abortion efforts here in Texas, lobbying at the capitol, repeating clever talking points to the media, and running an abortion clinic, I'd even aborted two of my own children. I felt like my sins were calling out to me, telling me how worthless I was. I worried about the fact that I still had no emotion about my own abortions, not even since the ultrasound-guided abortion. There was something wrong there, like a hard shell wrapped around the memory of those events that could not be penetrated, just sitting in the pit of my soul like an anchor, holding me down. *What is wrong with me?* I drifted into a fitful sleep.

I awoke early Monday morning, October 5, with a feeling of weighty pressure sitting on my chest. I dreaded the thought of going to the office.

Doug did his best to cheer me up. "Let's just trust God, Abby. He's in this with us. You're looking for another job, leaving the clinic—making the right decision for the right reasons."

"But Planned Parenthood is all I've known for eight years! And other than the abortions, I love what I do, and I'm good at it. I love counseling women, educating them, getting them tested, running the clinic, motivating the staff, training the volunteers. But more than anything, I've always believed I'm making a difference in the world for good. Where do I go from here? And what are we going to do if I can't find another job soon? What about the house? Our expenses? What if this ruins us?"

"Don't try to solve our entire future in one day. We can't. Just focus on making right decisions for right reasons today. God will show us the way."

I didn't believe him. But I appreciated his encouragement, even if it was optimistic naiveté. That was just so Doug. I kissed him and left for work.

I approached the Planned Parenthood fence and drove through the open gate. It felt as if darkness were descending on me as I entered. Dread—that's what I was feeling. *Even though I'm now appalled at what happens inside this fence, I'm crossing through it as if everything is fine. But it's not fine. This is a death house. A prison. And I've been both prison guard and prisoner.*

The powerful thought shook me. *Get a grip, girl. Don't get dramatic. I'll get another job. I'll be gone by Friday. I can hold out until then.*

But when I checked my e-mail, my pep talk evaporated, replaced by intense frustration. Another e-mail from Cheryl reiterating that I needed to get my clinic's abortion revenue up. *She's relentless,* I thought. *I guess the reprimand in my file has given her even more power over me.* My stomach turned flip-flops as I reread the e-mail.

Enough. I closed my e-mail program and got up from my desk. It didn't help. At every turn all morning, the darkness was more evident. I looked into the waiting room and saw clients with sad lives waiting their turn for our help, and wondered if each of them was simply a dollar sign, a source of revenue, to this organization. A wave of nausea swept over me. I'd been a pawn in a game. Duped. Used. I reviewed the budget numbers and felt the flames of anger licking at me. The words I'd been hearing over the past few months replayed in my mind. *Nonprofit is a tax status, not a business status. Revenue per patient must increase. Abortion quotas have been raised. You've got to find a way to get your abortion numbers up. Get your priorities straight. We are building the largest Planned Parenthood center in the country, where we'll be able to perform late-term abortions. Increase the number of days each week for medication abortions and direct women toward that option. Beam me up, Scotty.*

I was having a hard time keeping it together. The images of the ultrasound-guided abortion kept replaying in my mind. Finally, tears that had been welling up—long overdue—spilled down my cheeks. I rushed back into my office and closed the door. I sat down at my desk and looked out the window. A client who'd just left the building was walking toward her car carrying a little brown bag.

Today is an abortion day too! The thought struck me like a slap in the face. *It's Monday. We're dispensing RU-486 abortions all day. Why was I thinking I had to be gone by Saturday? We're taking lives* today, *and I'm still a part of it. I'm still here!* I scanned my desk, filled with an impulse to pack it up immediately, and then my eyes fell on the small card from Elizabeth. For two years, that two-by-three-inch card with the soft pink tulip and handwritten note had been sitting on my desk in my little note holder. *Of all the cards I've received over the years,* I wondered, *why has that one remained front and center?*

"The Lord has done great things for us and we are filled with JOY."
PSALM 126:3

I am praying for you, Abby!
~ Elizabeth

I looked back out the window. There were two Coalition for Life volunteers standing on the other side of the fence, side by side, praying over this place. Praying. Simply praying.

I could hear Elizabeth's voice in my head, "We are here to help you. Let us help you." I'd heard them all say those same words a thousand times to every volunteer, every client, every staff worker, and to me. In that moment light broke through the darkness and I saw with such simple clarity.

I am on the wrong side of the fence.

I am on the wrong side of the fence!

I knew what I had to do.

They'll think I'm crazy, God—but if that's what I need to do, okay!

I didn't hesitate for a second. Tears were pouring down my face, and my heart was hammering. I grabbed my purse, opened my office door, and charged straight toward the back door of the clinic on the way to my car.

Megan saw me and called, "Are you okay?" She'd seen my face, my tears. I could hear her concern. But I couldn't stop.

"I just need to go. I'll be back," I called over my shoulder. I pushed the door open and jumped into my car. I didn't know who all had seen me, but clearly I hadn't made a quiet getaway.

"They'll think I'm a kook. They'll think I have lost my mind," I said as I started the car. "But I don't care." Tears blinded me; I had to wipe them away so I could see to back out of my parking place. But nothing would stop me now.

If I turned left, I'd be there in three seconds. *Better not go directly there. I don't want to cause a scene if anyone sees me driving straight to the Coalition house.* So I pulled out of the driveway onto 29th Street, drove about a half mile, then pulled into a parking lot to turn around, and headed back toward the Coalition for Life house. I pulled into their parking lot as close to the back door as I could. *What should I do? If I go barging in there they'll panic, thinking I'm on the attack.* Sobs shook my whole body. *I'll call them and ask if I can come in.*

I fumbled for my BlackBerry. I knew their number was 846-BVCL (for Brazos Valley Coalition for Life), but on my BlackBerry keypad, the letters aren't displayed next to the numbers as they are on a touch-tone phone. I couldn't figure out which letters would go with which number. Flustered, crying out loud, I tried through my tears to look up their Web site on my browser to find their number. Finally, I found it and dialed.

A young, sweet voice answered, "Coalition for Life. How may I help you?"

I was crying hysterically, and my words sounded choked. "This is Abby Johnson from Planned Parenthood."

A pause. Silence. And then I could hear caution in her voice. "Well, hi, Abby. I know who you are."

She must have been wondering what on earth was going on, because I was crying so hard I could barely get the words out. "I'd like to come in and talk to you guys. I'm out here in your parking lot. Can I come in your back door? I don't want anyone to see me."

Again a pause, and then, "Can you hold on just a moment?" I almost laughed in spite of myself because I could imagine the shock on her face. *What must she be thinking?*

When she came back on the line, her voice had gone really steady, like she was talking somebody down off a ledge. "Abby, this is Heather. I'm gonna open this back door now. You can come in."

I bolted out of the car and stood at the back door, looking over my shoulder as if I were being stalked. I heard her unlock it and realized they must have the same kinds of security issues we did at the clinic. But they didn't have a six-foot perimeter fence with security cameras. Their place looked approachable rather than being fenced off like a prison. The building was a ranch house, probably built in the early 1950s.

The back door opened into a small sitting room. Standing just a few feet away were Heather and Bobby. They looked terrified, as if I had a bomb strapped to me. They simply stared with a deer-in-headlights look, totally still, while I stood there, body shaking with sobs, dressed in black clinic scrubs, mascara running down my face—just a mess. An absolute mess.

"I want out," I blurted, "I want out. I just can't do this anymore." More sobs wracked my body. I had no idea what I'd really come to say and no idea what I'd say next. The only thing I knew for sure, and I was now very sure of it, was that I had been on the wrong side of the fence and had to get to the right side.

Their jaws dropped. They looked at me, then at each other, dumbfounded at seeing the director of the clinic their organization had been protesting for twelve years standing before them, sobbing, undone. Totally undone.

Then Heather stepped forward, put her hand tenderly on my back in a gentle caress, and whispered, "Here, Abby, come sit on the couch." Her simple kindness unleashed more sobs from deep within—a place so deep I didn't even know it was there. And yet I did know. A dam deep inside of me had broken, and a torrent of guilt, grief, pain, remorse, shame, secrets, and fear was bursting out of me with every sob. It was a horrible, wonderful, frightening, cleansing gush of raw emotion. As I sat down, I noticed that Karen, another young volunteer, had entered the room too. All three looked at each other and me with puzzled expressions: *Is this a scam? Has something happened? Someone died? Some terrible accident? What's going on? Is this for real?* I didn't blame them. What else would they think?

I didn't see Shawn, and oddly, I was sorry he wasn't there. *What's that about?* I wondered.

Karen sat down beside me on the small couch, her long, wavy brown hair spilling over her shoulders as she leaned toward me. She was petite, with deep brown eyes and dimples, and she looked like the picture of wholesome innocence. I'd seen her many times at the fence. Her eyes were filled with compassion.

Heather offered me a box of tissues and then lowered herself into a chair across from me. She, too, was petite, with long, straight blonde hair and beautiful blue eyes, now huge with an expression of bewildered wonder. I remembered shooing her out of the flowers by the fence one day when she'd been talking to one of my clients and how she'd shrunk back from me when I'd reprimanded her for it. I was pretty sure that Elizabeth, the one who'd given me the card on my desk, had trained Heather as a volunteer counselor about two years ago.

Bobby went to the kitchen and got me a glass of water while I blew my nose and wiped my tears, hopelessly smearing my already running mascara. Then he sat down on the floor directly across from me. He had always exuded a friendly, clean-cut, affable persona that had appealed to volunteers on both sides of the fence. He had short dark hair, dark brown eyes, and a square jaw. I felt like he was sizing me up, trying to figure out if this was all a ruse of some sort. The room wasn't more than eight feet across; I realized that it must be their counseling room, where they bring women looking for help—some of them women who'd first come to Planned Parenthood but had been drawn, instead, to the fence counselors by offers of help. It was homey and comfortable in soft earth-tone shades, and I felt myself relax a little. I took some deep breaths that still rattled with involuntary weeping, though it seemed to be quieting now, and took a few sips of water, trying to regain my composure. Then Bobby broke the silence.

"So tell us what's been going on, Abby." He said it so gently, with such kindness, that I started crying again.

But between the sobs, the words began pouring out of me. "I know what I've been doing is wrong. I mean, I didn't used to think it was wrong, but now I do. About a week ago I had to help with an ultrasound-guided abortion, and I saw the whole thing—this perfect little body and how the baby tried to get away and then violently twisted, and I saw the body crumple, just crumple, the little spine just sucked away and . . ."

The story came out in a rush, a flood. I babbled on for a few minutes. Karen cried with me. Heather looked horrified and heartbroken. Bobby looked at me with a mystified expression, part empathy and compassion, part suspicion and distrust. They all three moved in closer, leaned toward me, and listened as I spewed out the bottled-up thoughts and feelings that had been simmering for years, mounting over the past months, and exploding over the past week.

"Shawn just pulled up," Karen said after about five minutes.

A strange sense of relief surged through me. I even managed to laugh a little through my tears. "Well, maybe you'd better go brief him. If he sees me sitting here, he may have a heart attack." All four of us laughed nervously.

"Do you want him to know you're here? Do you want him to come in?" Karen asked, standing.

Did I? I realized that, yes, I wanted him to be a part of this. For eight years we'd been kind of like captains of opposing teams, both on this journey, facing off through the fence. "Yeah, I'll talk to him."

Shawn had gone straight to his office. Karen told me later that when she said, "Abby's in here, Shawn—I think you need to come," his jaw had clenched. Perhaps he expected to hear that a volunteer had done something stupid and that Abby was on the warpath.

"Why is she here?" he asked.

"She says she saw an ultrasound-guided abortion," Karen explained. "She's telling us she wants out of Planned Parenthood."

"Abby? And she wants *me* in there? What do you think—will I help or hurt?" He was already following Karen out of his office, but clearly he was trying to process the absurdity of what he'd just heard. "Okay, yeah. I'll talk to her."

I heard him coming behind Karen.

I'll never forget it. Shawn stepped into the doorway, looked at me, paused, then slowly leaned against the doorframe as if he were casual, relaxed. He smiled, tilted his head, just taking me in. Here I was on his turf, undone, my puffy face with smeared makeup, a pile of tissues on my lap, his team huddled around me. I could feel him sizing up the situation.

"Tough Monday?" he asked, grinning.

And just like that, the reassurance of his open, hopeful, grinning face made me relax. I laughed, even as fresh tears began pouring down my face.

"You could say that." I grinned back at him, exhaling, laughing, crying. I looked around me at the three volunteers I'd been opposing through the fence all this time. And then back at Shawn, my counterpart across the fence.

I felt my tension melt.

"Yeah. You could say that."

CHAPTER FIFTEEN

Open Arms

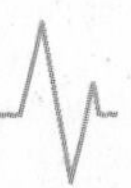

SHAWN WAS GRINNING EAR TO EAR. He stepped out of the room and came back with a chair, joining our circle. He looked around the room, and we all looked back. He could see that Karen had been crying, that Heather was overcome with emotion, and that Bobby was mystified, cautious, maybe suspicious, but hopeful, too—Bobby with his open face.

"So what's going on, Abby?"

I was reassured by Shawn's presence. These other three were so young, so new to the movement. Not that I was that much older—they were in their early twenties, and I was closing in on thirty. But Shawn was about my age, and I'd considered him my peer on the other side of the fence. I thought about the two of us starting as volunteers within a month of each other, and now we were both leaders in our movements. Neither of us would have dreamed of this scenario. The others had been caught up in my emotion that afternoon. But Shawn seemed calm, self-controlled. It was soothing to have his steady presence in the room.

He listened. I talked. And talked and talked and talked. I described the ultrasound-guided abortion, every detail, and he kept his steady eyes glued on mine. My guilt, my new understanding of Planned Parenthood's real priorities, how I felt duped and used. The pressure I'd felt to increase revenue and abortion numbers. My tensions with Cheryl, my love for the work I'd been doing, my disgust over the huge Planned Parenthood center being built in Houston, which might eventually provide abortions all the way up to twenty-four weeks. My fears about losing my income, about my career and future. My attempts at job hunting. My concerns that I'd never be able to get another job in conservative, pro-life Texas with "abortionist" tattooed on my forehead.

"But I still believe in birth control," I announced, as if someone had challenged me on it. They hadn't, but for some reason it was important to me to say it. "We've got to help women avoid unwanted pregnancies. That's critical to reducing the number of abortions!" I announced it like I was stumping for election.

"Hey, we're not trying to convert you," Bobby replied. I realized he wasn't sure I was sincere. He looked guarded, like maybe I wasn't for real. I couldn't blame him. I thought of all the accusations and tensions we'd shared across the fence for so long. The media statements I'd issued accusing them of harassment, painting a picture of them victimizing my workers and clients. Why should he believe me? I wouldn't if I were him!

Then I realized it didn't matter. He didn't need to believe me. None of this was about what they believed. I hadn't come to convince them of anything. I'd come because I'd had to. Because I'd wanted out. Because I finally knew I was on the wrong side when it came to really helping women in crisis. Because God had called me to come. It was as simple, as unplanned, as spontaneous, and quite frankly, as crazy as that. I didn't have the slightest idea what was to come next. I hadn't decided I was now pro-life. I hadn't come to join their movement. I only knew that I had to come here.

Someone asked what got me involved to begin with and I told them my story. It was cathartic. The more I talked, the better I felt, so I kept talking. I unloaded thoughts and feelings that stretched over my entire eight years at Planned Parenthood. I found myself spilling out thoughts and feelings I'd been afraid to admit even to myself or to Doug. Every now and then, Shawn or one of the others asked a question or slowed me down to try to make sense of my torrent of words, but for the most part, they just listened.

And then my cell phone beeped. Suddenly fear hit the room.

Shawn looked at his watch. "How long have you been here?" he said. "Do they know where you are? Were they expecting you someplace?" He looked alarmed, as did the others.

I pulled my phone out of my purse. It was Doug.

"Hey, Doug. You are never going to believe where I am." I sounded happy! I could actually hear it in my own voice. It was the weirdest thing.

His answer blew me away. "At the Coalition," he answered with barely a moment's hesitation.

"What! How did you know? How could you possibly guess that?" I held the phone away from my face and just looked at it a moment in disbelief.

"I don't know. It's just that, with all the conversations we've had and all that's been going on, I just thought that maybe one day you'd reach out to them."

Doug, my naive (or so I'd thought) optimist. He'd known.

Heather asked, "What'd he say? How'd he know?"

"He says he just kinda figured that one day I'd reach out to y'all. How could he possibly know that?"

"I always knew I liked Doug," Heather quipped. Knowing she'd never even met him, we all laughed. We laughed like old friends. It felt good.

"So what's next?" Doug asked. I could hear his voice trying to break through our laughter.

"I . . . well . . . I don't know yet," I answered. And I didn't.

"I left the office. I'm sure they just think I went out to lunch. Oh my gosh, lunch! I was supposed to have lunch with Megan. I'll call you back."

I had tons of text messages and began reading them. They were from Megan and a few other girls at the office.

"R U OK?"

"R U coming back?"

"What's wrong?"

"What R U doing?"

"R we having lunch?"

They went on and on.

"They want to know where I am," I said. "Am I still coming for lunch? Am I okay?"

"How long have you been gone?" Shawn asked again.

"Over an hour," I replied. I couldn't believe it had been that long.

"Won't that make them suspicious? Abby, do you need protection? Do they know you came here?"

Karen looked anxiously toward the back door and windows. Bobby got up and looked out a window.

I could imagine what was going through their minds. Had

someone seen me come? Had they called the police? The Coalition for Life was about two weeks into the 40 Days for Life campaign. Would my situation become a media circus? Was someone going to come bursting in, accusations flying?

Bobby looked at his watch. "I've got to get to the fence. I've got someone scheduled for sidewalk training. I'll let y'all know if I see anything suspicious." He got up, then said, "Abby, I don't know if this is appropriate or not, but can I give you a hug?" I stood up, and he gave me a warm embrace, then left.

"No one knows I'm here," I said to the others. "They'd never understand. I need to leave soon and have lunch with Megan."

"Abby, we can help you find a job," Shawn said. "We've always told you we were here to help. We'll help you or anyone at the clinic who wants to leave. We're going to help you get out. We mean that."

"Are you serious?" I asked. "You'd really help me?"

"Right away. I'll start making calls today."

"Dr. Robinson," Heather said.

"Right," Shawn answered, "we've got someone you just have to meet. Dr. Haywood Robinson. Over at the Med. I know he'll help. He'd love to. He's been right where you are."

I knew of Dr. Robinson. He and his wife had once been prominent abortionists. Then they'd had a dramatic conversion. They had left their abortion practice years before and had become outspoken pro-lifers. He was an influential man in the Texas pro-life movement and served as a physician at the local College Station medical center, known as the Med.

"Can I call him, Abby? Will you agree to meet with him tomorrow? I know he'll make time for you. Can I call him today?" Shawn sounded like a kid begging for a trip to the candy store.

I was stunned at how quickly the tables were turning. I'd come here a blithering, emotional mess, literally running away from Planned Parenthood into the camp of "the enemy," and now they were offering to begin a job hunt for me, today. They were embracing me as a friend. Offering to help. And, I realized, I truly *needed* their help. I'd crossed the border. There was no going back, except to extract myself. I had no idea what was next, but Shawn, who now seemed like my big brother, protector, and advocate, was already forging a new path for me.

"Yes. I'll meet with him. And yes, I do need help finding a job. We depend on my income. I can't stay at Planned Parenthood—I know that now. But I can't leave, either, without a job. If you think you can help, I'm ready."

Shawn surprised me with his next comment. "Abby, how about if we pray for you. Could we do that?" And before I knew it their heads were bowed and Shawn was pouring out his heart to God, thanking Him for the work He'd been doing in my heart, praying for me and Doug and Grace, asking God to give me wisdom and truth and insight.

I felt the presence of God—felt the connection I'd been longing for over the past few years. I knew I was in the presence of Almighty God, and once again the tears flowed—more deep, cleansing tears. But they were not tears of grief and remorse this time. They were tears of relief, of awe. They took turns praying for me. I'd never experienced such an outpouring of personal, dynamic prayer. By the time the prayer ended, I was sure I'd gone through nearly the entire box of tissues.

"Okay. You get back over there. Go to lunch. Lie low. I'll call Haywood and make some other calls. Don't worry, Abby. You're not alone in this. We're here for you."

I believed them.

They really had been here for me all along, just like they'd been saying through the fence for eight years.

I quickly texted Megan, "I'm coming back. OK." Then I went into their restroom to try to fix my face. I really was a mess. But I got myself together. They gave me a little tour of the house. The front room was very welcoming and homey. It had green walls and a dark wood floor, comfy chairs and off to the side an old but charming cherry desk, like a receptionist's desk. Behind the desk was an entrance to a large conference room, which they ushered me into. There on the wall was a huge banner with a gigantic photo of a baby inside the womb, his eyes closed, his little hand near his mouth, and next to him in large letters "beingHuman." I recognized it as the promotion poster for the *beingHUMAN* documentary Shawn had taped at my old church, and I remembered how he'd protected my identity from my pastor when he could have outed me.

Clearly this was the headquarters room, with a huge whiteboard covering an entire wall, filled with the schedule for all the volunteers walking the fence for the 40 Days for Life campaign. So many names. I was in the enemy camp for sure, and the photo of the baby resonated within my heart, reassuring me that this was, indeed, the right side of the war.

The small but comfy kitchen led to the small counseling room we'd been in, and a hallway led to what had been designed as two bedrooms, but were now two offices—one Shawn's, the other a shared common office.

They all gathered around me in the hallway and hugged me. Karen wrote down her personal cell number and pressed it into my hand. "Call me if you need anything, anytime." It was a huge step of personal trust, and I knew it. I caught Heather's expression of surprise, followed by a huge affirming smile.

Then Shawn led me out the back door. It was almost comical—he was looking in all directions like a secret agent, peering around the corner of the house, making sure no one was watching for me to come out. It would have seemed silly, except that we both knew that our war came with death threats and extremists on both sides. We were aware that many people would feel suspicion and alarm if they spotted me leaving Coalition for Life's headquarters. I climbed into my car. They were waving good-bye. I waved back and made a left, followed by three more lefts, and pulled back into the Planned Parenthood lot. All the way around a big block when only one hundred steps, if that many, would have taken me door-to-door.

CHAPTER SIXTEEN

Keeping Confidence

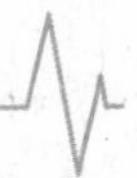

I DROVE INTO THE PARKING LOT at the Planned Parenthood clinic, pulled out my cell phone, and called Megan. I took a deep breath and tried to sound as normal as I could.

"Hey, Megan, let's go out to lunch."

"Are you okay?" she asked. "Where did you go?"

"I'm fine. Just come on out and let's go."

One minute later she was in my car. She took one look at my face and said, "Abby, what's wrong?"

Megan and I had been friends for a long time. True, I was her supervisor at work, but we'd traveled together, gone to church together, hung out apart from work. I trusted Megan. So I said, "Megan, I'm going to tell you something, but you have to keep it quiet. Okay? You *have* to." She nodded.

"I'm going to leave Planned Parenthood. I have to get out. I just can't be part of this place anymore." I told her why. Finally, I told her I'd just been over at the Coalition for Life.

To my surprise, she laughed. Not a mocking laugh, but as if she just couldn't believe it. She didn't sound or look nearly as blown away as I'd thought she'd be. She asked if they were going to help me.

"Yes, they are. They were . . . they were great. Really great. I mean, they were supportive and just happy that I came to them. No judgment, no condemnation. You know they've always said they'd help us. They've offered again and again. And they just seemed excited to be able to help. They were ready to make phone calls on my behalf today, to help me find another job. It was amazing."

Megan nodded, thought for a moment, and then asked if I thought they would help her, too.

My heart leapt. "Absolutely! I know they would! It's what they want." I was amazed that she was showing this much interest so soon.

When she asked what she'd need to do, I told her just to get her résumé together. She said she thought she still had the résumé she'd submitted before joining Planned Parenthood the year before. She'd update it and then give it to me so I could pass it on to Shawn.

I was so excited for her! She was a nurse-practitioner, and I remembered a conversation we'd once had when she told me that she disliked the abortion part of our operation. She did Pap smears and ultrasounds and served as a clinician seeing patients, all of which she'd told me she enjoyed. But on abortion days, she started IVs and administered meds. She stayed in the room for abortion procedures until they were complete.

"Let's go to lunch," I said. "I'm starving."

After we ate, we both came back to the office excited. She asked for a copy of her job description, which I gave her, and I decided to give her a copy of my evaluation of her work as well. It had been very positive, and maybe she could use some of my comments about her good work on an updated résumé. I handed it all to her, and she said she'd work on her résumé and e-mail it to me.

Then I thought of Taylor, for whom I'd always had a soft spot. Taylor was a terrific health care assistant, compassionate and caring. She mostly interviewed patients before they went to the examination room. She was valuable to the clinic, but for some reason I always felt that she needed me to take her under my wing. I would no longer be able to do that, of course, if I were leaving, so I decided she needed to know. I called her into my office.

I told her my story, told her what had happened to me earlier that day. Her response was similar to Megan's. She was surprised, first of all, to hear that I'd gone to the Coalition for Life office, but she said she understood. She didn't like abortions either, but she cared about our patients. She asked if I thought they'd help her find a new job. Now that I was leaving, she'd like to get out too.

When I said I knew they would, she asked if I'd help her with her résumé, since she'd never done one before.

I told her I'd be happy to. I asked if she'd like me to make a copy of her job description to help with her résumé. She said yes, so as I had for Megan, I copied Taylor's job description and evaluations. She thanked me.

When I called Shawn to tell him about Megan and Taylor, he was surprised and happy. The Coalition for Life had been offering help through the fence for so long, and suddenly he had not just one but three people ready to take him up on his offer. That the three of us were coming to him during the 40 Days for Life campaign made it all the sweeter. He also reminded me he was going to set up a meeting to introduce me to Dr. Robinson.

I couldn't believe how fast everything was happening. I looked at the clock. It had been only a few hours since I'd run out of the clinic in tears, and now Shawn and his gang were checking out jobs around town for three of us. On top of that, Shawn was making an appointment for me to meet, of all people, a well-known pro-life former abortionist. What a bizarre turn of events.

My homecoming to Doug was strangely wonderful that evening. I still couldn't get over the fact that he'd guessed my whereabouts earlier in the day. We were both so lighthearted compared to that morning, when he'd almost needed to push me out the door with his assurances that God would show us the way. He just grinned as I recounted the conversations I'd had at the Coalition for Life and with Megan and Taylor. I was talking a mile a minute, exuberant with relief. Like me, he was blown away by how quickly everything had changed.

"So what's on tomorrow's agenda?" he asked.

"Well, I'll go into the office in the morning. I still have the rest of this week to work there. Shawn said he'd let me know when he nails down an appointment with Dr. Robinson."

We were both nearly giddy. It looked like such smooth sailing from here. Of course, the question of income still hadn't been solved, but we'd seen God at work in such obvious ways that we felt confident it was all in His hands.

And today that was true. It *was* in God's hands. But Shawn, Bobby, Heather, and Karen had a more accurate picture of what was about to unfold. I didn't know it until Shawn told me later, but their afternoon would end in a far different tone than mine.

I'd no sooner waved good-bye and driven out of the Coalition for Life parking lot than Shawn closed the door, turned to his team, and said, "Everything that just happened stays in this room, right? No one tells anybody. Understood?" Karen and Heather nodded. "Not even the board. We need to make sure she's safely away from Planned Parenthood before this gets out."

"She was so open with us, so trusting. You don't think she'd trust the folks at Planned Parenthood like that, do you?" Karen asked.

"She probably will," Heather said. "I mean, that's Abby, isn't it? We've watched her through the fence long enough to know that she just tells it like she sees it. What you see is what you get. Whatever she thinks, she says. It's hard to picture her keeping this under wraps at her office."

"This is so exciting! It's unbelievable!" Karen said. "Of all people, Abby Johnson. The clinic director! Remember all those prayers? And Elizabeth, the burden she always felt for praying for Abby. She was always hopeful. She always said, 'Abby's there doing what she believes is right. One day she'll see the truth.' Remember?"

Shawn nodded. "I know. It's incredible. And I really want to enjoy this moment and celebrate and offer thanks, but guess what? My mind's going a mile a minute. Planned Parenthood is going to come after her, and us. I just know it."

Bobby came in, back from his sidewalk training. "Is she gone?"

"Yeah, but you should have seen her face," Karen said. "The joy. The transformation. Did you see it, Heather?"

"I feel kind of guilty," Heather said. "I was really suspicious at first. I mean, I *wanted* to believe her, but I was just afraid to believe it was real."

"I thought the same thing," Bobby said. "Remember David Bereit a few years back telling us about that time one of the Planned Parenthood staff expressed to him that she was fearful of the pro-lifers, so David gave her his cell number so they could keep in touch—and then for weeks he got all those prank calls and finally had to change his number? And then that same woman *teased* him about it later, through the fence, and said he was so gullible. That's what I was thinking about when Abby first started out. But the more she talked—well, I watched her face as she described the ultrasound-guided abortion. You could see the pain. The remorse. The guilt. It was all real. But I've got to be honest—I'm still on my guard."

Shawn said, "When this gets out, and it will, people will ask us to vouch for her. Everyone in town knows she's part of Planned Parenthood. Lots of people won't consider her for a job unless we stand behind her. So we'd better all be on board in trusting her. But my biggest concern right now is for Abby. I have a feeling that you're right, Heather. She'll trust her friends in Planned Parenthood because she believes they *are* her friends. And she'll get burned. They'll come after her, I know they will. And us, too. I'm picking out my tie already, 'cause I know I'm going to end up in court over this."

"Maybe it won't get that far. This wouldn't be the first time they served you with papers. There've been, what—three other times? All on trumped-up charges, and none of them made it to court."

"True, but this time they're going to believe some kind of conspiracy is at work. I mean, this time it's *Abby Johnson*, for goodness' sake. The director! And she isn't just leaving. She came to *us*!" Shawn shook his head.

Bobby asked Heather, "Did you tell them about when Abby drove up?"

"No," said Heather, laughing. "I haven't had time. You guys won't believe it. I was sitting in the back office and saw a little red car just like Abby's pull up in the back, and, joking, I yelled, 'Hey, Bobby, I think Abby just pulled in!'"

"Yeah," Bobby said. "I wasn't paying any attention. I just figured she was fooling around. So I said, 'Mmm. Okay. Whatever.'"

"And thirty seconds later the phone rings, and it really is Abby, asking if she can come in. I about dropped the phone! I froze. I had no idea what to do. I put her on hold and walked into Bobby's office, and said, 'Bobby, Abby Johnson really *is* in our parking lot, and she wants to come in the back door.'"

"What did you say?" Shawn asked Bobby, laughing hard now.

"You should have seen Heather's face!" Bobby said. "She was white as a ghost, and I swear she was shaking. And I said, 'Well, don't just stand there—invite her in!' And we both braced ourselves for some barrage of complaints. I was thinking, *Oh, great. What did some volunteer do now? Did Abby call the police? This has to be bad.* So by the time Heather unlocked the door, we were both just standing there, ready for anything, expecting really horrible news. And there was Abby, not on a rampage, but on her escape! Unbelievable."

After the four of them had had a good laugh and shared their thoughts about what I'd done and said, Shawn sobered them all back up. "Look, guys, I know we've got a lot to celebrate, but we've got to be careful now. With the 40 Days for Life campaign going on, the media and police will both be on high alert. Once Planned Parenthood gets wind of Abby's plans to leave—and knowing Abby, she'll be the first to tell them, and it won't take long—I think they'll be looking for a fight. They'll want to hurt her and us. So we don't say a word. Don't even tell any of our other volunteers."

I wish Shawn had been wrong. But he couldn't have been more right.

By the time the four of them had finished their conversation, I'd probably already told Megan, and maybe Taylor, too. After all, they were my friends. I trusted them.

CHAPTER SEVENTEEN

The Right Thing to Do

EVERY FRIDAY MORNING, Shawn met Dr. Haywood Robinson for breakfast. Their friendship had been built over years of working side by side in the pro-life movement. Haywood and his wife, Noreen, both African American physicians, had been abortion doctors before a dramatic conversion experience, after which they'd became fierce pro-life advocates. Shawn, who was Catholic, and Haywood, an evangelical Protestant, served as brothers in the cause for life.

I hadn't been gone from the Coalition for Life house more than an hour before Shawn dialed Haywood at his office. "Hey, brother. I've got something for you. You'll love this!" Shawn filled him in, then said, "I'd like to bring her to see you soon to talk about helping her find a job, and I know you'll want to get to know her."

Haywood was gracious and said he'd be delighted. They agreed to a meeting at 1:00 p.m. the very next day, Tuesday, October 6.

Tuesday morning I was dancing around the house as I got ready for work. I'd awakened feeling ten times lighter than the morning before. Light enough to float to work. It wasn't that I didn't feel the anxiety of being about to walk away from my career; I did. Doug and I were both a little anxious about my being jobless for a while. But that felt like a small burden compared to the huge burden I'd given up yesterday. My defining wrong-side-of-the-fence moment and my obedience to God in simply getting up and crossing that fence had broken through years of torment, guilt, ambivalence, and confusion. A high, thick wall that had been standing between me and God was obliterated. In its place, I felt a river of joy flooding in. I'd never felt this way in my life.

I drove to the office, waving at some who were praying at the fence as I went through the gate. I enjoyed their baffled looks as they tentatively waved back.

While I was doing paperwork at my desk about an hour later, my cell phone rang. Caller ID told me it was Shawn. That was a first—Shawn calling me at the clinic! I closed my office door and answered. Shawn whispered through the phone, "It's Shawn. Can we talk?"

"Yeah, what's going on?"

"You're sure it's okay? Nobody knows, right?" Shawn was still whispering.

I wasn't. "Yeah, it's fine. I really don't care who knows!"

"Well, you need to care, Abby. Don't go announcing, 'I'm done with this place. I'm having a meeting with Haywood Robinson and Shawn Carney.' Okay? You need to be careful. Don't underestimate the repercussions of this. I want to make sure you hear me on this, Abby. Be careful."

"Okay. I get it. Where should I meet you? And I'm in my scrubs. Is that okay for this meeting?"

"Yeah, that's fine. It's at a hospital. You'll fit right in." Shawn suggested a spot and confirmed 1:00 p.m. I giggled as I hung up. I felt like we were playing spies or something. I simply felt so lighthearted.

I quietly pulled Megan aside and told her about the planned meeting with Dr. Robinson. She asked me to find out if he had any openings for nurse-practitioners.

I left the office at lunchtime and met Shawn in the parking lot at the Med. It was a gorgeous fall day, clear blue sky, seventy degrees. Shawn was wearing his 40 Days for Life shirt. Some spy!

"Nice shirt. Very inconspicuous. So if we run into somebody who recognizes me and they see you with that shirt, you don't think they might be suspicious?" We both laughed, and he agreed he was not cut out to be a spy. Not exactly CIA material.

"Nice name tag," he shot back. And he was right! I had my Planned Parenthood name tag on my scrubs. I think we were both surprised at how comfortable we felt with each other, as if we were old friends.

"You are beaming. Just beaming, Abby." And I knew I was. I could feel it.

Shawn didn't usually meet Haywood at his office, and he didn't seem sure of the way. Before long, we were totally lost. And we started to laugh. And the more we laughed, the harder we laughed, like a couple of kids on a lark. We went down one hallway, then another, reading signs and backtracking. We even stopped once to ask for directions. We thought we were following them until the hallway ended in a door marked, "Emergency exit. Alarm will sound." We burst out laughing.

"Listen," Shawn managed to say, "the two of us *cannot* get

arrested together in this town! Here we are, the directors of these two vehemently opposed organizations. Can you imagine the headlines if we set off the fire alarm at the hospital?" We both cracked up. Sheer silliness.

Finally, we found the right elevator, and a woman entered with us. Shawn, Mr. CIA, was trying to stand in such a way that she couldn't see the logo on his shirt, which, of course, drew her attention to it.

"What is 40 Days for Life?" she asked.

Shawn, without missing a beat, turned to me and said, "Would you like to answer that?" I burst out laughing again. I can't imagine what the lady thought.

But Shawn said, "It's a forty-day prayer and fasting campaign where we go to abortion clinics and pray for people, even those who work in the clinics."

"Well, that's a really good thing," she replied. The elevator stopped at her floor and she walked out. Clearly she hadn't noticed my name tag.

"Guess I'd better take this off, huh?" I laughed as I tucked my name tag into my pocket. The elevator stopped again, and we got out.

We finally got to Haywood's office, and the receptionist led us back. When we walked into the handsomely appointed office, there was Morgan Freeman! Well, not really, but Haywood looked amazingly like him. I noticed right away that he was wearing the Precious Feet pin, a favorite among pro-lifers. I held out my hand for a handshake, and the next thing I knew this tall, distinguished man was saying, "Come here, dear," and he wrapped me in a warm hug.

I felt an instant bond. *He's been there,* I thought. *He's been in my shoes. He knows.*

He invited Shawn and me to sit on the couch with him, and Haywood and I began sharing our stories. I can't describe the hope that filled me during that visit. He, too, had done the unthinkable. He told me of the years he and his wife spent in the abortion industry, then how they'd had a personal encounter with Jesus, committed their lives to following Him, and subsequently abandoned their abortion business to join the pro-life movement. Now here he was, an advocate for life, helping others. Truly helping them. Moving them toward life, always life. Never death. Something stirred deeply inside of me. I wanted to do that too! I wanted to always be on the side of life. I wanted to bring that kind of hope and help to women in crisis. After a while he said, "Let's pray together."

He opened the door and beckoned a young woman in from another office. She may have been one of his nurses. To her he said, "This is Abby. I can't tell you what's going on with her, but she's got issues, and she needs prayer right now."

He turned to us and said nearly the same thing about the young woman. "This girl has been through a lot. I won't go into details, but I'm so proud of her. She's raising a young son. She just made the decision to go on to medical school, and Noreen and I have been encouraging her."

Next thing I knew, we were praying. Haywood prayed with power and passion, and then the nurse prayed, and Shawn prayed. I wanted to pray but couldn't speak. I was crying again.

When we opened our eyes, everyone looked at me.

"Every time we pray, I cry," I said. And everyone laughed a warm, understanding laugh.

Then Haywood gave us a note to take down to HR. I told him about Megan.

"Have her send me her résumé."

At HR, I handed the note to the woman there, who said, "Oh yes, Dr. Robinson called down and said you'd be coming." She handed me an application, which I filled out.

We made our way back to the parking lot, making only a few detours this time, and stood there in the brilliant sunshine.

"I've got to go out of town tonight," Shawn said. "I'm speaking at a 40 Days for Life event in Dallas. But you know my cell. Call 24/7, for any reason. Anything, okay? The team is still making calls. A job will open up. I'll be back in a few days."

I knew what he was wondering. Finally he asked, "So what are you going to do?"

"Do you think I should just go ahead and resign?" I asked him. The answer was obvious. Timing was really my only question at this point. But I wanted to know how he'd respond.

"Look who you're talking to," he said, pointing at the logo on his shirt and smiling. "Of course you need to resign. I know you don't have another job yet, but God will provide. He provides for these situations. And you will not have to worry. It will all get taken care of. He is faithful."

"I *am* going to resign. Today. Because it is the right thing to do."

He threw his head back and laughed, nearly shouting, "Because it's the right thing to do! Yes! Because it is the right thing to do!"

He looked like a little boy, caught up in the total joy of the moment. He grabbed me and hugged me, nearly dancing with excitement. If I'd known then what Shawn knew, if I'd had any idea of all that had gone on behind the scenes since 1998 at Coalition for Life, or even in the past twenty-four hours, I imagine I would have exploded with joy right there on the spot. It would be a while before I would discover the rest of the story. But I knew this much:

I knew that somehow, as great as my joy was, Shawn's seemed even greater. I could see right down to his heart, and it was marvelous to see.

I did know what that moment meant for me. I was taking a new stand, beginning a new life.

Eight years before, I'd stood at a volunteer fair, a naive and impressionable college girl, and I'd heard a plea to join a cause to help women in crisis and decrease the number of abortions. I'd taken a stand that day, one I'd thought was the right one, and signed up for Planned Parenthood. I clearly remember thinking, *This is where I am planting my feet!* I had decided on the spot, in the Texas A&M Flag Room, *I can make a difference here. I can help prevent unwanted pregnancies, make abortion rarer, and help women who need help. This is good for women, good for the community, and perfect for me.*

It had taken me eight years to discover that by aligning myself with an organization that performed abortions, I had condemned myself to be part of the very thing I'd said I wanted to decrease. Since that decision, it had been a long, slow slide into darkness. It was all so clear to me now. I'd lived in that darkness for eight years, and in it I'd lost my day vision. I had harbored my own dark secrets. I had built fences that separated me from my parents, my husband, my friends. I'd fenced myself off from my own conscience, leaving me adrift and confused in shadowy places. And I had fenced myself off from the connection to God that I longed for. Today peace was flooding in, washing away the rubble of that shattered fence.

That day, October 6, 2009, I planted my feet on the right side of the fence—the side of life. Standing in the parking lot of the hospital that afternoon, I knew I was doing more than just leaving Planned Parenthood. I was joining the pro-life movement.

Shawn and I hugged good-bye. "I'll text Bobby that you're leaving today so that he'll watch out for you. What time do you think you'll tell them?"

"I'll wait until the end of the day, around 4:30. That will be the least disruptive for everyone. In the meantime, I'll type up my resignation."

"The team will be there for you, Abby. And we'll all be praying."

As I floated back through the clinic gate at about 2:30 p.m.-and I truly felt like I was floating—I knew it was my last time through the gate. This time, instead of feeling darkness descend upon me, I was carrying light inside the place with me. What a difference.

I was grateful for the light, because as I walked into the clinic, the reality, the implications of what I was about to do hit me with full force. I saw the women in the waiting room and wondered what would become of them. Without me here, would the abortion numbers at this clinic skyrocket? The patients were so vulnerable, so easily swayed. To me they had always been individuals. But now I believed that to the organization they were dollar signs. Some clients came back periodically—I'd gotten to know them, shared life-altering moments with many of them. I'd miss them. I'd worry for them.

I saw my colleagues. These were women I loved. Almost every one of them was here out of compassion and the desire to make the world a better place by helping women in crisis. We had shared so much together. *They will never understand,* I thought. *They will feel betrayed. There may never be a way to reconcile with them once this is over. I won't be welcome here ever again.*

But the light was in me, carrying me. I knew I was following

God, that He was calling me to follow Him, and it was the right thing to do. I would just have to trust God to take care of what was beyond my control.

I had about two hours and lots to do. I made a mental checklist. *I've got to pack up everything that's mine. I've got to write my resignation letter, gather everything that belongs to the clinic—keys, access cards, everything—and leave it all for Cheryl. I don't want to walk out of here with anything of theirs, and I don't want to leave anything that's mine because I know I'll never come through these doors again. But first, I have to do the hardest thing of all. I have to tell some of my colleagues in person.*

I started with Megan, then Taylor, telling them both of my meeting with Dr. Robinson and Shawn and my decision to resign immediately.

Megan was sad, surprised at how quickly I was leaving, but she understood.

Taylor seemed more distressed. "Don't leave us here, Abby, please," she said. "Wait until we all have another job lined up." But I assured her we'd all be job hunting together, and I'd do all I could to help her find a new job fast.

The others I told one by one, a few by phone, with no mention of my contact with the Coalition for Life. I explained that Cheryl and I had been increasingly at odds because she wanted to take the clinic in a different direction than I did, that Cheryl had instructed me to increase the abortion numbers and I was not willing to make that a goal, and that she told me abortion was to be my priority—and it never would be. I explained that I just couldn't stay any longer under those circumstances.

I packed up my office, finally removing my photos of Doug and Grace from my desktop, and last of all, the note holder with

Elizabeth's card. *I'll take this home and frame it,* I decided. Then I typed up my resignation letter.

At precisely 4:30, closing time, I faxed my resignation letter to the HR office in Houston. I left my keys and access cards in the appropriate place for Cheryl to find the next day, knowing that in the wake of my resignation she'd be here in a hurry. I felt so clean. So right. I couldn't have felt better.

I put all my belongings in my car and then remembered, of all things, my vacuum cleaner. It was an extra I'd had at home, and I'd brought it into the office a while back for us to use there. I didn't want to leave it behind. It was the last thing I carried out of the clinic. I exited the building through the door used by staff, past the privacy gate on the side of the building. I heard the gate clang to a close, and when it did, I had the oddest momentary reaction. Suddenly, I panicked. I was now locked out. No pass key. No reentry. My former career was now locked in that building, and there was no going back. The finality of it struck me, at first as fear and then as a wave of relief.

Megan and Taylor were waiting by my car in the parking lot as I approached, lugging my vacuum cleaner and wearing a silly grin at the thought of what a bizarre scene I must be making. They wished me well and hugged me good-bye. We were the last ones there. Then, on the other side of the fence, I spotted Bobby, standing on the grass, just as Shawn had promised. There was another Coalition for Life volunteer standing next to him, watching everything, clearly bewildered. I waved at Bobby and pointed to my vacuum, laughing. He laughed too. I couldn't imagine what the poor volunteer thought. Bobby waved back, and to my surprise, Megan and Taylor waved at him too. *Well, there's some hope!* I thought. *Maybe they'll soon wind up on the other side of the fence with us.*

I caught myself. *Us?* It surprised me to realize that I was already seeing myself as part of the Coalition. The bond had grown so much in just one day.

We climbed into our cars, and I followed Taylor and Megan out of the gate.

That closes eight years of my life, I thought. *That ends a career. But that is now in the past. The future God wants for me is straight ahead.*

As I drove past Bobby, I smiled and waved again. I watched in my rearview mirror and saw him fall to his knees with his hands lifted heavenward. Still praying at the fence, but this time, I knew, praising instead of pleading. I was praying, too, and it felt wonderful to be praying *with* him.

And, of course, I was crying.

Every time we pray, I cry.

CHAPTER EIGHTEEN

Facing Forward

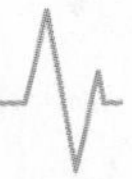

I CALLED MOM THAT NIGHT. In fact, I could barely wait to tell my parents about my decision to cross the fence and walk into the offices of the Coalition for Life, and that fact alone was a warming internal affirmation that I was following the path God would have me choose.

So on Tuesday, October 6, my parents got the call from me they'd probably been praying for ever since they'd first learned I was working for Planned Parenthood. Doug and I had just put Grace to bed, and I curled up in my favorite chair and dialed their number.

"Hi, Mom. I've got some huge news for you. Can you get Dad on the phone, too?"

Knowing that my mom can always tell my emotional state by the sound of my voice, she had to know I was happy. As I'm writing this, it occurs to me for the first time that maybe they thought I was calling to tell them I was expecting! I'll have to ask her.

"I resigned today from Planned Parenthood," I told them. You could have heard a pin drop. I hadn't told them about the ultrasound-guided abortion one and a half weeks before, so they'd been in the dark about my inner torment since that day.

"I have a lot to tell you." And so I did. The cleansing I'd experienced the day before in my figurative leap over the fence, and now the bold steps today of meeting with Dr. Robinson, then resigning, had been so monumental that I'd wondered how I'd ever convey them to my parents. But once I got started it seemed effortless. The words and emotions came pouring out. As always, my parents listened with love, asked a few questions, and let me know they were there for me.

"You've done the right thing, Abby," Mom told me. "I've been praying you'd leave there for so long. I am proud of you."

"Are you okay on money? Do you need anything?" Dad asked. I teared up, touched that no matter what I'd ever done in my life, my parents were always ready to support and help. Wasn't this just like Dad? His first response was to make sure his little girl's needs were taken care of. And then the thought hit me: God, my heavenly Father, was always looking out for my best interests too. Though I surely deserved to bear the consequences for my actions, He'd provided the right people at the right time to encircle me with love and support. I pictured Bobby, just today, on his knees, arms lifted, right outside the fence. God was answering the prayers of many—and I didn't even know how many—in leading me out of Planned Parenthood. The step I'd taken today wasn't an isolated event that was all about me. It was one scene in a much larger story.

It would be a while before I discovered the true scope of that story.

Shortly after I hung up with my folks, the phone rang. It was Shawn, calling from Dallas to check in on me.

"So how are you holding up?" he asked. "How did it go this afternoon?" I filled him in on the details, then switched gears.

"Shawn, I am dying to talk to Elizabeth. I just have to let her know the part she played in all of this, the seeds she planted two years ago with those flowers and her card."

"Maybe you'd better let me call her first," he suggested. "I'll let her know what's happened and that it is for real."

I agreed, but as the night wore on I couldn't wait. I looked up Elizabeth's e-mail address on the 40 Days for Life Web site and e-mailed her, telling her my story and ending with, "This really is for real. You can call Shawn if you want to verify it."

The phone rang again. One of my colleagues from another clinic whom I had called earlier that day with news of my resignation was on the line. She told me that she was worried about her job, now that I'd confided in her about my decision to leave. She thought Cheryl would be angry to discover that she knew about my resignation before Cheryl did. She asked if I would feel betrayed if she called Cheryl that night to tell her.

"You can call and tell her whatever you want," I answered, finding myself surprisingly relieved at how free from fear I felt over Cheryl's possible reactions. "If you feel you need to tell her in order to cover yourself, go ahead."

I was relieved now that I hadn't told this colleague about the Coalition for Life—I'd told no one but Megan and Taylor about that. My resignation was one thing, and obviously, by the next morning Cheryl would learn it along with everyone else at the Houston office. But my joining the Coalition—I needed some time before word got out about that. It would be so easy, given all the mutual suspicion of both organizations, for such news—the news that I'd visited the Coalition the day before I resigned and spent time with Shawn the very day I'd resigned—to spark worries that I'd been feeding information, or conspiring in some way, with *either* organization. I thought of Shawn's warning to keep it quiet and lie low. He was right.

By the time I crawled into bed that night and curled up next to Doug, I felt like a new woman. I was exhausted from all the emotion of the past few days and the mammoth decisions I'd made in such a short period of time, but it was a wonderful exhaustion. *This must be what a runner feels after completing a marathon,* I thought. *It must hurt all over, but the exhilaration of finishing the race makes all the pain worth it. That's just how I feel!*

The next morning I got a call from the same colleague. She gave me a detailed account of her conversation with Cheryl. I wish I could say that I was satisfied with what she said and didn't want to know more. But it wouldn't be true. I knew that high drama would be unfolding throughout the day—and in all likelihood the next week—and I was curious. So as the phone continued to ring that day, I ate up every piece of news. Megan called. She'd taken the day off, but Cheryl had called her several times asking her to come in and asking if she knew anything more or had noticed any suspicious behavior from me. Taylor called too, describing how Cheryl had met with each employee separately, trying to piece together who knew what and when, asking if anyone had noticed me cleaning out my office or taking things home. Nothing surprising, of course. It didn't worry me. I'd been careful to clean out my belongings and leave things in excellent order.

Megan, it turns out, was using her day off to work on her résumé. She e-mailed it to me the same day, and as Megan had requested, I forwarded it to Shawn.

Shawn called me as well, and I confessed I'd already e-mailed Elizabeth. Just then his phone beeped at him. "Hey, this is a call coming in from Elizabeth! Hang on." He only had me on hold for a minute before he came back on, clearly elated.

"Abby, she's so excited she's crying. I'm going to fill her in and call you back." Only a few minutes went by before my phone rang again, this time from Elizabeth. We both wept as we talked, marveling at how God had worked. I did my best to express my gratitude for how she'd reached out to me and loved me, even though I was running an abortion clinic, which violated what she believed in. We planned to meet for lunch a few weeks later when she'd be able to drive to Bryan.

For the rest of the week I continued my job hunt, now free to network with anyone who came to mind. I set up a few interviews for myself. Other than that, I enjoyed being home with Grace and digging into some projects around the house. I felt so free.

Sunday morning, the first Sunday since my resignation, was a day of spiritual celebration. This time, as I prayed the confession, I was filled with gratitude and awe at how God had moved me, led me, and loved me through the ordeal. I thought that maybe this gave me a new insight into how Moses might have felt after he led the Israelites out of Egypt. Free at last!

As it turns out, I was about to find myself trapped between the Red Sea and the chariots of Pharaoh.

Fortunately, ignorance is bliss, so I enjoyed my victory celebration.

Taylor called again to let me know she had decided to resign very soon. She'd been trying to work on her résumé so I could give it to

Shawn. Then she asked if she could come over after work one night so I could help her finish it.

I told her to come over. I was eager to see both my close friends on the staff get out of Planned Parenthood and find the same release I was experiencing.

We worked first on her resignation letter, then on her résumé. It was fun seeing her prepare to make this step and doing what I could to help. We spent hours on it and finally, around midnight, finished it up and e-mailed it to Shawn. She thanked me and headed home.

She called me the next day to tell me she'd decided not to quit until she had a new job lined up. I could understand the concern.

"That's fair. Come on over again tonight. I'm filling out some online applications. I'll help you fill out some too. Let's see how fast we can find you a job."

We worked long hours again that night, mostly working separately on our own applications, although at her request, I helped her fill some out. We sent them all off that night, and once again, with thanks, she left.

The next two weeks were wonderful. I went for a few interviews and was encouraged by several possibilities. Most days Taylor, Megan, and I texted or called just to check in with one another on how our job hunts were going.

Meanwhile, in those two weeks, my bond with the Coalition for Life was growing stronger. I was on the phone numerous times with Shawn and his team. I had what seemed like hundreds of questions about prayer, God, the Bible, and the Coalition's stance on medical ethics. Just a flood of questions. They were eager to answer and wanted me to know they were praying for me. They also kept me updated on job possibilities. I also asked about their work—their goals, how they trained volunteers, and what services they offered to women who came to them in crisis.

The more we talked, the more I came to understand that their vision for providing care and resources for these women was incredibly similar to my own, but that their vision to truly care for a woman went far beyond her immediate circumstances. They cared about each woman as a whole person—an *eternal* person—in the context of her family, her spiritual needs, her long-range physical and emotional health. They offered solutions that would enhance a woman's life over the long term.

This difference in perspective led me to much self-examination. I thought of my efforts at the clinic to increase adoption as an option and how life-affirming that choice is, not just for the child, but also for the birth parents, who would know they'd taken the challenging yet right road of carrying their child to term and then entrusting that child to a family longing to nurture him or her. I thought of the inner strength that builds in birth parents, which then becomes a success story in their lives. I considered mothers who decided to parent rather than abort—their choice to sacrifice career and financial comfort in order to invest themselves in their children. Such decisions are hard, but I could see the good that God would do with such strong and brave decisions.

I was beginning to grasp what seemed to me a stark contrast between the Coalition for Life's mind-set of life-nurturing, long-range solutions versus Planned Parenthood's more immediate focus on solving short-term crises. Pregnancy and STDs were problems to be "solved" by abortion and medication—even though those solutions often left the root problems in place and exposed women to great risk. The more I learned, the more my eyes were opened to a brand-new way of seeing how God was working through the Coalition to truly change lives.

My Coalition for Life friends continued to network for me, getting the word out that I needed a job. Shawn connected with a local doctor who supported the pro-life cause and expressed interest, so Shawn invited me to drop by the Coalition house to talk about it. I was glad for the invitation. I knew we wanted to be careful about keeping me from being spotted, but I also found myself drawn to spend time with these new friends. Shawn filled me in on the pro-life doctor and his clinic. It sounded quite positive, so we agreed I'd give him a call. But something was bothering me, and I couldn't hold it in any longer.

"Shawn, I need to tell you something." He looked concerned, deadly serious, and leaned forward. His eyes got huge, like he was afraid I was going to tell him I was heading back to Planned Parenthood. I felt a little nervous but went on.

"I am really struggling with something. I feel like an imposter. I realize what abortion is and the evil that it is. I know I've left the abortion clinic and I'm never going back. I know I don't ever want to have anything to do with the abortion cause again. But I've got to be honest. I am not sure I am really . . . well . . . quite what you'd call pro-life yet. I find it hard to even say the word, Shawn. It's weird, because I know I'm on my way to being pro-life, if that makes any sense, which it probably doesn't. But I'm really struggling over some of these issues. Do I really think abortion should be illegal? Well, I believe now that it is not the moral thing to do, but illegal? Should it be a crime? Will that really keep women from aborting? I know it won't, and I know illegal abortions would just skyrocket. And what about rape and incest? Even if abortion were to become illegal, wouldn't I still support it in those cases? I've got so many unresolved questions."

Shawn looked at me for a moment, then threw his head back and laughed out loud. He wasn't mocking me, and I knew he wasn't belittling me. But clearly, he was amused—the last response I ever would have expected to my confession. He leaned forward again and I had no idea what was coming.

"You know, Abby, you were running an abortion clinic just two weeks ago. Two weeks! If this is Abby Johnson's biggest struggle right now, we're doing pretty well. We'll get to that. It will come with time. Your life has just been flipped upside down by the Holy Spirit. You're going to need to rethink everything you know and prayerfully discern what is true and what is a lie. That will take time and prayerful silence before God. I suggest you not rush to resolve your internal arguments but dive into prayer and allow God to finish what He has started."

I sighed with relief, and he turned back to his computer. He grinned and then mumbled to himself, loudly enough so I could hear, "Abby Johnson is not pro-life enough for herself. I love it!"

My gratitude to the Coalition for Life was beginning to prompt some deep introspection, driving me more and more to prayer. Frankly, I'd always been an action kind of person. But now I was in a period of stillness, of waiting, though I wasn't sure exactly what I was waiting for. I only knew it was time to wait on God. The physician Shawn had connected with set up a time for us to meet, but not for another week. I wasn't worrying about that, though, which reassured me that God must surely be in control, because I knew that on my own, I'd have been anxious.

One Friday evening, October 23, about 9:30, I was in the shower, praying. I found myself praying at all times of the day and night, truly enjoying my new sense of fellowship with God. I suddenly had an urge to go to the clinic fence and pray. At first, I dismissed it. Shawn and I had agreed that I should keep my distance from the clinic. We still didn't want word to get out that I'd joined the Coalition for Life. Our inclination was to let some months go by, then ease me slowly into volunteer work at the Coalition. Otherwise, my sudden shifting of sides might attract accusations of conspiracy. After all, paranoia and distrust ran wild on both sides.

But the urge to go pray at the clinic fence was persistent, and I began to believe that it was from God. And just that fast, the thought of my own two abortions invaded my mind. I looked at my hands and once again thought how culpable I was for the deaths of more babies than I knew. Tears sprang to my eyes and mingled with the water from the shower coursing down my face. *Go to the fence and pray.* I felt compelled.

"If there's one thing I should know by now, it's that when God tells me to do something, I should do it," I muttered. "But what will Doug think?" I toweled off, threw on a T-shirt and workout pants, and, hair still dripping, walked into the living room. Doug was sitting in the recliner.

"You're going to think I'm crazy," I announced, "but I need to go to the clinic."

Doug looked at me, perplexed. "Are you going to vandalize it?"

"No, I'm not going to vandalize it!" I scolded. Good grief, the poor guy didn't know what to expect from me these days! "I'm going to pray."

"Oh. Abby, I don't think that's crazy at all."

So we agreed he'd stay home with Grace. We kissed good-bye and

I left. It was 10:00 p.m. We both knew that the 40 Days for Life campaign was still going on, which meant that at least two people would be praying at the fence. I was nervous. What would they say?

I need to call someone. I thought of Elizabeth. We'd spoken several times since my e-mail to her the night of my resignation. *Yes, I need Elizabeth!*

As I dialed her number, I started to cry. "I'm going to the fence to pray," I said when she answered. "Do you think that's weird?"

"Sounds to me like God is calling you there, Abby. I think it will be healing."

"But Shawn told me that some of the volunteers have noticed that my car hasn't been there, and they're wondering where I've gone. What happens if I show up and people recognize me?"

"Just tell them the truth." Elizabeth made it sound so simple. I talked to her until I parked.

Two young students praying at the fence looked at me as I approached. The night was dark, but the streetlight was bright and they could see me clearly. Not sure why, I walked up to them.

"Hi," I said tentatively. "My name is Abby Johnson. I used to be the director of this clinic, but just about two weeks ago I resigned. My conscience wouldn't let me stay. Please don't tell anyone you saw me, but I just had to come here tonight to pray." It felt so cleansing to say it.

The two hugged me. "That's wonderful!" they said in unison, grinning from ear to ear.

I stepped off by myself. I closed my eyes and faced the building. I knew I needed to face this place. I had to face what I'd done. I had to acknowledge the part I'd played here. It was here that I'd aborted my second child. It was here I'd escorted women into the hands of Planned Parenthood. It was here I'd casually scheduled the deaths of countless children. I took a deep breath and opened my eyes.

I was standing face-to-face with my sin, embodied in that building. I allowed myself to feel the weight of it. I had to own it. And I did.

Sometimes, words fall too short.

I will say this. Good Friday has never been the same for me since.

Jesus took upon Himself the weight of the world's sin on the cross. I cannot fathom such a weight. Yet I had a sense of the weight of the lives of my two unborn children and thousands of others I had willingly forfeited at the hands of an abortionist.

But Christ didn't stay on the cross. *He arose.* And that is what I experienced that night. Once I truly owned the weight that night, I gave it to Jesus Christ at the fence. And He lifted it off my shoulders and off my soul.

As I looked upon the building between the bars of the fence, I knew that it was here that God called me out. I was not only facing the place of my sin. I was facing the place of my deliverance as well.

I prayed. The sounds of the busy street at my back faded away. I heard only silence. I was alone with God, communing with Him, meeting Him here in this place. Peace enveloped me, and I knew it was the peace that only God can give.

At the fence, beyond a shadow of doubt, my healing had begun.

On Wednesday, October 28, Taylor had an interview scheduled at a medical clinic in town. She called me later that day and asked, "Want to have dinner with me?" We met at a Mexican restaurant. Over dinner, she excitedly filled me in on her job search and talked about her desire to go on to nursing school. While we were at the restaurant, we both got text messages from Megan. She'd had meetings at the Houston office with other Planned Parenthood nurse-practitioners, and she'd ridden there and back with Cheryl. While they were in the car, Megan had received a call from someone who was considering my application and was calling her as my reference. From her text, I got the impression Megan found this funny, and Taylor and I shared a laugh over it.

I needed to get to choir practice at my church, so we prepared to go our separate ways. After hugging me good-bye and promising to call the next day, Taylor told me that Barbara, along with the CEO of the Planned Parenthood affiliate to which the Bryan clinic belonged, were coming down the next day for their annual planning meeting. She said she hoped it would be her last meeting. "It won't be the same without you," she called as she climbed into her car.

I smiled. I felt so free no longer having to wrestle with my conscience or the budget crunch and mandates and priorities of Planned Parenthood.

I didn't hear from Taylor or Megan the next day, Thursday. I assumed their meetings had run late and didn't give it much thought. I texted both of them but didn't hear back. Friday, all day, I expected a call or text from them, but nothing.

Then Friday night, while watching a movie at home with Doug, I got a call from a good friend who worked in another Planned Parenthood clinic. She was one of the few I'd called the day I resigned, just to give her a heads-up so she'd hear the news directly from me rather than through the grapevine—though, of course, I'd not mentioned anything to her about the Coalition.

"Abby, I have a question for you. Are you working in any way with the Coalition for Life?"

The question startled me. I'd been very careful not to mention my connection to the Coalition to anyone, and I knew that Shawn had stressed secrecy to his team. I wondered what her source was, but her question was direct and I wasn't going to lie.

"Yes, I've been talking with them." I held my breath, waiting for her reaction.

"Okay, Abby. Well . . ." I assumed the long pause was because she was trying to decide how to respond to what I was sure was not the answer she'd been expecting. "Well, when I'm not legally bound to Planned Parenthood anymore, I'll call you back and ask you more about that."

"Okay, sure," I responded. She quickly said good-bye and hung up.

Well, that's really weird, I thought. *No longer legally bound? What on earth does that mean? Does it mean that Planned Parenthood knows about my connection to the Coalition for Life? She actually sounded scared.*

I dialed Megan, wondering if these two days of silence from her and Taylor were connected somehow.

Her cell phone number was no longer in service.

"What?" I asked aloud. Was something wrong with my phone?

"What's wrong?" Doug asked.

"Can I use your phone?" I asked Doug. "Something weird is going on."

Using Doug's phone, I called Megan again. The same recording.

I explained it to Doug, then said, "Maybe it's a phone service issue. Megan has an out-of-state area code. Maybe she switched over to a new service or number."

So I called Taylor's number.

It, too, was no longer in service.

I felt the air being sucked out of my lungs. Something ugly was about to unfold.

Dear God, I prayed, *what's happened with my friends?*

CHAPTER NINETEEN

The Injunction

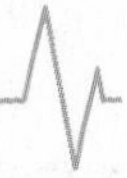

AFTER THE PHONE CALL from my colleague from the other clinic, I was sure everyone at Planned Parenthood, all the friends and coworkers who'd been my daily companions for years, now knew or would shortly know that I'd defected—that I hadn't just left Planned Parenthood, I'd joined "the enemy," the Coalition for Life.

When I'm no longer legally bound. My friend's words were echoing in my thoughts.

I knew this organization well. Terribly well, with an emphasis on "terribly." I'd seen firsthand how quick they were to take legal action. I thought back to my earliest days at the clinic, before I'd become director, and recalled that their first course of action, whenever they felt they had the slightest justification, seemed to be to call the police. As an organization, their practice, by my observation, was to look for any opportunity to draw media attention that might make them seem the underdog. I felt a wave of shame that I'd been a part of their efforts, as one of their media spokespersons, spreading their talking points every chance I was given. Some kind of litigation was coming down. I could smell it.

Worst-case scenarios flew through my mind: Would I need a lawyer? Would Doug and I lose everything paying for my defense? I could just imagine Doug standing there, forlornly watching the police haul me away in handcuffs to serve out some unjust sentence, and the bank foreclosing on the house we lost in our vain attempt at my defense.

God is in control, I reminded myself. *Trust Him.*

I texted Shawn: "The cat's out of the bag. I think they know."

And I didn't have to wait long. His text came back: "Yeah, I know. Just don't say anything else. And our attorneys . . . " And his text stopped there! He'd run out of characters! What a place to stop, mentioning attorneys! In my frame of mind, already imagining all kinds of legal repercussions, he mentions attorneys.

So I texted him back: "WHAT!!!!!!!!!!!!!!!!!!" Just basically sitting on the exclamation point, making sure he got the message.

A short time later, though it felt like hours, he called, explaining why he hadn't been able to call immediately. When I'd first texted him, he'd just finished a family shopping trip and had been in the parking lot of a grocery store, crammed in the back cargo section of their SUV, which was filled to overflowing with their three kids in Halloween costumes, Marilisa, and his mother-in-law. I suppose if I'd stopped to think, I'd have realized that since it was the evening of October 30, Halloween was the next day, which is a big deal when you have young children.

"So you see, Abby, since we're still keeping quiet about everything, I couldn't talk about it in front of my mother-in-law." He told me Marilisa had sensed something was up, so the two of them exchanged eyebrow signals in the rearview mirror as she drove home with Shawn squeezed between the grocery bags in the back. He had called me right after he was finally able to fill her in.

I understood the explanation, but his tone sounded so lighthearted that I assumed he didn't understand the seriousness of the situation.

"Shawn," I said, "I just found out that somehow Planned Parenthood knows I am now associated with the Coalition. I know Planned Parenthood. I think they'll come after me now with legal action of some kind."

"Yeah," he said, laughing, "I think so too." Laughing! I couldn't believe it.

"What's so funny?" I said. "Don't you realize how serious this is? They're going to take me to court! And what did that text mean, 'I know.' You already knew? When were you planning to tell *me*?" And that just made him laugh even harder, but believe me, this was no laughing matter. My heart was pounding, and it wasn't from joy.

Shawn then told me what he knew. Planned Parenthood was going to initiate two actions against us, probably on Monday. There would be a lawsuit and a temporary restraining order—basically a way to try to force us to keep quiet about everything that had to do with Planned Parenthood.

I asked him how he knew that much, and he told me that a copy of the temporary restraining order had been faxed to the Coalition for Life office that very night, since they were named as a defendant along with me. Unfortunately, only the first two pages had come through, so we didn't yet have the full document.

"What are we going to do, Shawn?"

"Well, first of all, there's not a lot we *can* do immediately since it's Friday night. They're no dummies. Their timing is deliberate—we have to just kind of cool our heels over the weekend and can't do much of anything until Monday."

"Can't we even—"

"Abby, try to calm down. I believe God is going to work everything out just fine. I've already talked to Jeff Paradowski, an attorney and friend, and he's going to represent Coalition for Life in this action, and he's also willing to represent you. So even though you didn't know you were getting served, you already have an attorney lined up. How about that?"

Yeah. How about that? If he'd just found out, how had he secured an attorney already?

"Shawn—I don't know what to say. An attorney? Don't they cost a lot of money? I just walked away from my job, remember? I don't have any money!"

"Jeff isn't doing this for money, Abby. He's a supporter. A friend. He's doing it for the Coalition for Life. He's doing it to help fight abortion."

Shawn went on to explain that when the office alerted him to the fax, as he sat crammed in with the groceries, he'd texted Jeff: "Planned Parenthood director quit a month ago, is coming to us. We've been served with papers. Need help."

And Jeff's reply, which has now become near legend in our group, had been immediate: "I'm in, baby!"

All of this had happened just moments before I'd texted him. I thought of the verse in Isaiah 65:24: "Before they call I will answer; while they are still speaking I will hear."

Shawn went on reassuring me that everything was fine, no problem. He'd already spoken to Jeff before calling me back. Jeff would represent us and we'd win, he said, and on and on. Frankly, I admit I suspected Shawn was making it all up as he went along because he hadn't had much more experience with this kind of thing than I had. Maybe he was just trying to calm me down. And I needed calming down.

But of everything he said, the one thing that did reassure me was knowing that we had an attorney. Someone who knew what he was doing, someone to whom this world of lawsuits and injunctions and courtrooms was his day in, day out job. That's definitely what I needed, and now that's what I had. I decided I could take Shawn's word for it that this guy knew his stuff. He told me some of the things Jeff had done, some of the cases he'd won, and it sounded impressive to me. I thought, *This guy Jeff sounds confident, and he sounds competent. Okay. This is good.*

One other thing reassured me: Shawn sounded very confident and impressively relaxed. I trusted Shawn, and if he wasn't worried about this, then maybe I didn't need to be either.

Well yes, I did. Who was I kidding? I was petrified!

Shawn was right that there wasn't much we could do until Monday. But there was one thing I could do—pray. I prayed all weekend that my friends Megan and Taylor had not been the ones to reveal my connection to the Coalition for Life, even though deep down I knew they must have. I hoped instead that Planned Parenthood had found out by some other means. In any case, it seemed that they had been forced to clam up. Perhaps the organization had made them turn off their cell phones, maybe by threatening to fire them or press legal action against them. Most of all, I prayed that neither had said anything untrue about me. I needed desperately to believe that, whatever had brought about this legal action and whoever had been behind it, it had not been a personal betrayal by Megan or Taylor.

I prayed for that, I hoped for that, but I also feared I had been betrayed. Otherwise, wouldn't they have called or been in touch? The silence from their end was deafening. And it did not bode well.

I had lots of time to think about things over the weekend, because basically that's all I did. And I cried. I cried all weekend. I was nervous, but as nervous as I was about the pending court action, there was something else I was even more afraid of.

I was afraid of finding out for sure that my friends, friends who had asked me to have the Coalition for Life help them find new jobs, had betrayed me.

Suspecting it, thinking it was likely, was one thing. Finding out for sure was something else, and I was terrified of how it would feel.

When I'm nervous, I have trouble sleeping. I wake up early, maybe 5:00, and can't get back to sleep. My stomach gets uneasy, tied in knots, and that's how it was all weekend. Doug and I went to church on Sunday morning, but I couldn't concentrate on the sermon, couldn't make my mind focus on what was being said because I kept thinking about Megan and Taylor and about the papers I would receive. What would they say? What would it mean for Doug and me?

Sunday evening, around 8:30, the strangest thing happened, the last thing I would have expected. Shawn called and said, "You won't believe this. A reporter with KBTX television just called. She got a press release directly from Planned Parenthood saying that they're serving you and Coalition for Life with a lawsuit and a petition for a restraining order. KBTX wants to know if we want to make a statement."

I could feel the blood draining from my face. "You're kidding."

"Nope. Isn't that a kick? They file for a restraining order against us to keep us quiet—and then they issue a press release to create news about it? What kind of sense does that make?"

I was speechless. But I was pretty sure I knew the kind of "sense" it made to Planned Parenthood. It created an opportunity to make news as the apparent "victim" of pro-lifers, it could intimidate their opponents, and it could either rally or intimidate their own staff. It also immediately poisoned my reputation, which could blunt any influence I might have were I to speak out about their internal agenda.

"So," he said, "you want to make a statement?"

"Well—I guess. I mean—we'd better, hadn't we? If they're going public with this thing? We both know, of course, that the restraining order doesn't take effect until a court official formally serves us the papers—right? And that hasn't happened yet."

"You don't have to convince me. I already told the reporter to meet us at the Coalition office in thirty minutes!" I could hear the smile in his voice, and I was beginning to catch a bit of his amusement in this process.

While I'm recoiling in anxiety as this drama unfolds, afraid of what is coming next, Shawn is celebrating and watching as God reveals His plans. He's trusting that God has a plan and is simply waiting on God to lead the way, knowing he will gladly follow. Maybe that's what comes from years of serving God so deliberately. Is that what it could be like for me?

In that moment I sensed a deep internal stirring, which I have since come to recognize as the whisper of God's Spirit. Something new was happening inside me. My faith was stretching, growing, widening, as if I were being given new eyes to see God at work. The best way I can think to describe it is to compare it to one of those nature films that shows a meadow changing over a season in ultrafast motion—where in a matter of moments we see a snow-covered field give way to greening, then wildflowers beginning to sprout, then an explosion of color and bees and hummingbirds hovering over a feast of nectar. We watch that all unfold in a matter of seconds, and suddenly we are blown away by the sheer magic of God's creation.

And it's not that we really learned anything new in such a moment. We already knew the change that happens over a season. But in normal time those changes are so tiny, so gradual, that they are invisible to us. Yet in high speed, when we can see with our eyes three months of changes in a matter of seconds, we are left in awe, stunned by the mystery of life sprouting from frozen ground into a magnificent nectar-rich canvas of color.

In that way I caught a glimpse of my spiritual life in fast motion. I saw myself grow from a little churchgoing girl to a teen who believed in and worshiped God to a college girl who abandoned God's standards of living and let my faith wither in neglect as I struck out on my own to save the needy, while God still nudged and whispered and called to me. In the blink of an eye I could see how God kept invading my life through parents who never stopped loving me, words of confession written centuries ago, worship services that kept calling me back to the foot of the Cross, deep disquiet in my soul that left me longing for God's peace, and . . . for eight years . . . faces and voices walking the fence, gently calling out offers of help, friendship, rescue, and the love of God.

And finally God put me face-to-face with the mangled brutality of the ultrasound-guided abortion, so I could see the destruction of life with my own eyes. At that point, God had finally broken through the wall I'd built. And once He had, I'd been undone to the point at which I'd looked out my office window and realized I needed to *run* to the life on the other side of the fence. And here on this side, God was now showing me, through circumstances beyond my control and through the faith of Shawn Carney, that I could trust Him.

I knew I was new at this trust thing. The difference between Shawn's reaction and my own was showing me that. But just like the fast-forward opening of a flower, I could see that my trust was beginning to blossom. God was doing His magic on me.

So around 9:00 that Sunday evening, Shawn and I met at the Coalition for Life house with the reporter and cameraman for KBTX. As we took our seats in the conference room, side by side, it dawned on both of us that this was our first official appearance in front of media representing the same cause, rather than opposite causes. The irony that it was Planned Parenthood who gave us this opportunity, thanks to their press release, felt like a gift from God and filled us both with a sense of God's commissioning of us to work together as a team.

We had no time for preparation. Lights were set up, the camera rolled, the reporter asked me to tell my story, and I simply answered her questions and recounted the events of the ultrasound-guided abortion and my decision to leave Planned Parenthood and come to the Coalition for Life. We expected it to air as a short piece on that night's news report. I called my mom on my drive back home to tell her to turn on the news.

"Mom, I think I'm about to be on the news. But I doubt it will be a big story, probably just something quick at the end." Mom turned on the TV while I talked with her.

After pulling into my driveway, I hurried into the house to tell

Doug and watch it with him. I was walking in my front door, still talking to my mom, when the 10:00 p.m. news program began. My jaw dropped. We were the lead story! Doug and I shared looks of disbelief.

"This is wild, Doug! My leaving Planned Parenthood is breaking news?" I threw my head back and laughed. "They really need to find some bigger news here in Bryan!"

There on every screen tuned into KBTX, Shawn and I were shown sitting side by side, and in the short excerpts of the interview they showed, I said, after a recap of the story of participating in an ultrasound-guided abortion experience, "I just thought I can't do this anymore, and it was just like a flash that hit me and I thought that's it."

Then I went on to say that I'd begun at Planned Parenthood, as many of my coworkers had, out of a sense of idealism and a desire to help women in crisis, but that it seemed to me the emphasis had shifted at the organization. "It seemed like maybe that's not what a lot of people were believing anymore because that's not where the money was. The money wasn't in family planning, the money wasn't in prevention, the money was in abortion, and so I had a problem with that."

The station had, of course, also contacted Planned Parenthood for a response, and a spokesperson had issued a statement that the TV report included: "We regret being forced to turn to the courts to protect the safety and confidentiality of our clients and staff, however, in this instance it is absolutely necessary."[15]

I had no idea, that Sunday night, of the chain of events about to unfold, thanks to that one press release from Planned Parenthood. When I revisit this part of my journey, I have to confess I simply laugh aloud and celebrate how God works, because that Planned

Parenthood press release opened a floodgate of media interest nationwide that accomplished the exact opposite of what Planned Parenthood had intended with this restraining order: It put my voice and the story of my change of heart as a result of that ultrasound-guided abortion before hundreds of thousands of people. It put that one experience of my moving from one side of the fence to the other at that clinic in Bryan, Texas, on October 5 into the national consciousness. You're holding this book in your hand because Planned Parenthood issued a press release on October 30, 2009.

At least, that's one way to look at it.

But the bigger story, the greater truth, is that you are holding this book in your hand because God is in the business of changing hearts and minds and using ordinary people for His extraordinary purposes. That night, when I saw what God had accomplished through the news story, the opening story no less, I found myself doing what Shawn Carney was no doubt doing that night—laughing with joy at what God was accomplishing.

As it turned out, I wasn't formally served the court papers until Wednesday morning. *Early* Wednesday morning—7:00 a.m. I'd just gotten out of the shower and was in my fluffy white robe with my monogrammed initials when I heard banging, and I mean banging, on the door. I nearly skipped my way to the door, and there stood a uniformed officer with papers in hand.

"Good morning!" I said with a big smile. "I've been expecting you." I remember sensing God's timing and control with great confidence that Wednesday morning because I had already seen the contents by then and already met with our attorney, Jeff Paradowski. Jeff's office had secured a copy from the court on that

Monday morning and e-mailed it to me and to Shawn. It had looked very scary when I'd first read it all, but exercising my new practice of recognizing God at work, I tried not to be too intimidated by it until I'd talked with Jeff.

The worst part of reading the papers was that they confirmed my worst fears. Among the allegations, the petition made it clear—if I chose to believe what it said—that Megan and Taylor had not just turned against me but had apparently given false statements to the court. According to the legal documents filed, Megan told them that I had given her résumé to the Coalition for Life without her permission. I can't express how badly that hurt.

But there in my bathrobe on Wednesday morning, face-to-face with an officer of the law who was holding out to me official documents whose contents I'd actually had since Monday, I was able to catch a glimpse of what God was up to.

The words I'd texted to Shawn on Friday night came back to mind.

The cat was indeed out of the bag.

And no one would be able to stuff it back in.

CHAPTER TWENTY

The Red Carpet

UNPLANNED.

Everything about my journey since running out of the Planned Parenthood clinic into the waiting arms at the Coalition for Life house was unplanned—by me, I mean. I look back on the journey and see God's fingerprints all over it, of course. If there is one seed I hope to plant in the heart of everyone who hears my story, it is this: God is worthy of our obedience and trust. When we step out in obedience, God rolls out the red carpet! That doesn't mean the path will be easy, but it does mean that He has prepared it for us.

I took great comfort in Philippians 3:13-14:

Forgetting what is behind and straining toward what is ahead, I press on toward the goal to win the prize for which God has called me heavenward in Christ Jesus.

I had no doubt that "forgetting what is behind" was going to be a challenge. I felt the weight of the part I'd played in furthering

Planned Parenthood's agenda for so long, and I felt foolish and used for not seeing the truth sooner. But I also felt the rush of excitement that I was now running a race for God. I'd lunged forward on October 5, when I'd literally run from my office desk to the door at the Coalition for Life, uncertain what awaited me, but simply knowing it was where God was calling me to go. Now, just a few weeks later, having experienced the bright lights of the Sunday evening news camera and with the court hearing looming ahead, I became aware that this race had an audience, in spite of my attempts to keep it quiet. God had rolled this red carpet right into the public arena! And I have to confess that this part amused me to no end: He'd used Planned Parenthood's own tactics to do so.

The Monday morning following the news broadcast telling of my change of heart and my decision to leave Planned Parenthood and join the Coalition for Life brought an avalanche of media attention. By early that morning, calls were pouring into the Coalition office at an overwhelming pace. And I don't mean a few calls. Literally hundreds.

That morning, relieved that I no longer had to keep my relationship with the Coalition for Life a secret, I headed over to their office. I felt so free! For weeks I'd been longing to give back to them in some way. I was used to being busy and active, and the weeks of lying low had been difficult, even though I'd been treasuring the time with Grace. I arrived at the Coalition house at about 7:30 in the morning. Shawn, Bobby, and Karen were already there, talking about the newscast. I grabbed a mop and scrubbed some floors to make good use of the vibrant energy I felt. Shawn and I were scheduled to go to Jeff's office later in the morning, so I had time to pitch in around the place.

At around 8:00, Heather walked in. She did a double take. "Abby, oh my word! You look so beautiful! I've never seen you like this!"

At first I thought she was teasing, since I was mopping the floor. Then I realized that she meant it.

"You are positively glowing! You look radiant."

Karen, smiling, said, "You're right! She's not hiding anymore."

And I knew what she meant—not just that my hiding these past two weeks was over, but that my spirit wasn't in hiding anymore. I'd been freed up inside by God, released from hiding my soul in the guilt I'd privately been wrestling for so long. The joy I felt radiated from me.

They both hugged me.

And then the phone started to ring. Bobby answered the first call, and he'd no more than hung up before it rang again, and then it was like the entire place erupted. Between calls, they were grasping for paper to take more messages. Soon they started calling out things like, "It's *The O'Reilly Factor*. They want an interview. What do I tell them?" and, "Laura Ingraham is on the line!" and "Fox News wants an interview!" and "Mike Huckabee wants you on his show! And you're in the *Drudge Report*."

News stations, both TV and radio, from across the country were calling. The faithful Coalition for Life staff got a crash course in new terminology: listener base, requests for exclusives. It was mind-boggling. It was exciting and fascinating. But it was also humbling. I felt so small compared to my God who is so big. I knew more than anyone that I was no hero. Just the opposite, in fact. I had blood on my hands for who-knows-how-many abortions, and I'd been paid for my work. The true heroes were working at the Coalition. They'd been walking the fence in 100-degree weather and ice storms. They'd been standing and praying for untold hours over weeks, months, and years. They'd been speaking words of care and concern through the bars of the fence while Planned Parenthood—while I—had maligned them and mocked them. Yet God was thrusting me into the spotlight. He had chosen to demonstrate, through me, that He redeems the foolish, the broken, the sinful, and then uses them to accomplish His purposes.

Media requests weren't the only calls coming in. Women were contacting the Coalition for Life as well. Women who had experienced the pain of abortion themselves were calling in for counseling and to send their thanks to me for speaking out. They were telling of their guilt, remorse, and shame. They were insisting that my story was giving them hope that they could leave those things behind. Pregnant women were calling to say that, after hearing my news interview, they had decided not to abort. Women who'd visited Planned Parenthood clinics and had left determined never to return were calling to urge me to keep telling the truth. Clearly, my story had touched a nerve. God was reminding me that this wasn't about me at all. It was about Him, His purposes, His story.

Not sure what else to do, I started taking calls and accepting interviews.

A couple of days later, Wednesday, I was heading into the Coalition house when Mr. Orozco, the faithful ex-policeman who never missed his stand-and-pray hours on Wednesdays and Saturdays, saw me. He rushed over. "Abby!" he cried with exuberant joy. "Oh, Abby, I have been praying for you for so many years. It is so good to see you on this side of the fence! What an answer to prayer you are!" He hugged me, and I hugged him back tightly. This kind man had been praying for me for years. God had answered his prayers. I had no words sufficient to express my gratitude.

I thought back to my conversation with Elizabeth just a few weeks before as she and I were having our first lunch together. I told her how often I'd thought of her and the friendship she had offered and how her card had sat on my desk for two years and played a pivotal role in my decision that day to run to the Coalition house. I also told her of troubling thoughts I had of guilt and remorse.

"Abby, I can't believe how God answered our prayers for you. In such a bigger way than we'd ever dreamed! Who knew what would happen in His timing?"

"It's hard to wrap my head around it all. Elizabeth, you've got so much more experience than I do at following God. I'm feeling a bit overwhelmed by it all, and I'm afraid I'll mess up somehow." I felt myself tearing up, suddenly aware that I longed for Elizabeth to mentor me.

"Abby, you've been through a dramatic change in a matter of just a few weeks." Elizabeth spoke so gently that more tears started flowing. "It sounds to me like you are almost afraid to be still. But you must. God is working on you. You need to be quiet before Him and let His work take root."

I hated to admit it, but she was right. I was afraid to sit still too long, afraid of the guilt that sometimes whispered to me in the early morning hours. I was afraid of silence. I just wanted to be busy for God until the past faded away.

I had done my best to take her advice over the past few weeks. I stayed home. And boy, was it quiet! I didn't know what to do with myself. I cleaned the house top to bottom, cleaned out closets, played with Grace, fixed dinner for Doug, rented movies, and tried to rest. I prayed, prayed, and prayed some more. I read God's Word. I stopped by the Coalition for Life office a few times, but only briefly, as I was nudged to leave by Shawn and the team. I practiced being still before God—a new discipline for me. It felt foreign at first, but Elizabeth urged me to keep working at it.

So until the night of learning of the temporary restraining order, October 30, I'd done just what she suggested. Now, hugging Mr. Orozco, I remembered that conversation, and it hit me that God, once again, had planned my path. I'd needed that time to rest. And now, with media requests pouring in left and right, there was no time to rest at all! Elizabeth continues to be a mentor to me. We still talk on the phone nearly every day. She keeps me grounded, she prays with me and for me, and she reminds me daily that God loves me. She is a gift from heaven.

I called her that same Wednesday afternoon.

"Abby! I hear the phones are ringing off the hook over there! Are you going to accept all those interviews?"

"How can I not? God's the one rolling out the red carpet for me. The least I can do is walk where He leads, right?"

"It's your time, girl! You go!"

Meanwhile, Jeff kept me posted on his preparation for the hearing. He kept asking if there could be anything I might have forgotten to tell him, anything at all that would explain why Planned Parenthood would be willing to go to court for what was obviously, to him, a meritless case. I wracked my brain but could think of nothing. He and Shawn were reviewing everything they could think of that might give cause for Planned Parenthood to have named them as codefendants in the case, but like me, they came up empty-handed.

Shawn and Jeff weren't the only ones who were busy. The Coalition for Life team was still taking countless calls from media, but now they were referring them to a speaker's bureau, which, at Shawn's suggestion, I'd contracted to handle media requests for me. What a relief! They were experts at handling such inquiries, and we were all glad to shed that role. My calendar was filling up.

But others were busy as well—bloggers. Pro-choice and pro-life bloggers were having a field day over me. Accusations of conspiracies sprang up on both sides. Some claimed I'd been a mole for pro-lifers all along and intentionally spent eight years undercover to try to discredit Planned Parenthood. Others claimed my defection from Planned Parenthood was nothing more than a ruse, that I was just an unhappy employee who faked repentance in order to win media attention and speaking engagements. Some claimed that there had been no ultrasound-guided abortion, that I'd simply fabricated the story. At first I read them and gasped, ranted, and wept over the blogs. But within a few days I was able to take it in stride. God's path was before me, and I knew the truth, as did the people in my life who mattered. I couldn't control or even influence the rhetoric, so I prayed for God's grace to let it be. At least it kept me praying! And I was realizing daily how important it was for me to spend time with God one-on-one.

My Facebook and e-mail were overflowing as well, averaging upward of two hundred e-mails a day, almost all of which were either from women in crisis who appreciated my speaking the truth or old friends cheering me on for leaving Planned Parenthood and speaking out. I felt I owed them each a reply and would often be up until 1:00 a.m. writing personal responses to each of them.

Perhaps the saddest fallout from the media attention and blogging came from a direction I least expected: members of my own church. Doug and I had been attending for nearly two years now. This was, in fact, the first mainline denominational liturgical church we'd ever attended. The denomination took a pro-choice stance, no doubt one reason I'd felt comfortable giving the congregation a try after a previous church, which we had loved, had denied me membership given my job at Planned Parenthood. That had been a painful time for me, and when we began attending our current church, after Grace's birth, I'd been deeply moved by the confession of faith that was part of each service. In fact, I recognized now that the weekly recital of the prayer of confession in the liturgy had been instrumental in my wrestling with God over my role at Planned Parenthood.

Now I began receiving e-mails from members of our new church. A few from my congregation cheered me on. But others were very angry. They reminded me that our church was pro-choice, and more than one suggested I no longer worship there.

One Sunday after a media interview, a few friends came up to me, saying, "You did great." But a couple of people seemed standoffish. That's when I began to discover both the good and bad consequences of taking a stand, particularly one made public in such a visible way.

One fellow parishioner—a good friend—sent me an e-mail she'd written in what seemed to me a very cold tone. She said that even though it might appear that many members of my church supported my decision, in truth they did not. And she reminded me that the Episcopal Church—the denomination to which our church belonged—was pro-choice, not pro-life.

I replied, trying to explain myself, and she replied, but we made no headway on resolving the tension between us. I must admit I was feeling somewhat under attack at this point. It wasn't just the hostility I felt from my former colleagues at Planned Parenthood—

now I was feeling resistance and disapproval from some of my church friends.

I was heartbroken. How ironic, I thought. When I was pro-choice, my pro-life church wouldn't accept me for membership. Now that I was pro-life, fellow parishioners who were pro-choice were withdrawing their fellowship from me. While I acknowledge the right of any church to stand behind its beliefs, I struggle with how that happened in these two instances. I don't have a perfect solution to offer; I can only speak to how these incidents affected me—and how I suspect similar incidents likely affect others like me, or at least like the Abby I used to be.

When the first church bluntly and somewhat awkwardly told me I could not become a member, the church lost any opportunity to influence my outlook. I wish they had offered to dialogue with me about why they were so committed to their pro-life position and why they found my work at the clinic such an obstacle to my becoming a member. Or at the very least, I wish they would have expressed care for me apart from my pro-choice position. Now some members in the second church were making me feel as if I wasn't even welcome in the building. A few went so far as to suggest that I leave.

In both instances I felt rejected. That's why I appreciate the fence-prayers' approach and encourage churches and other organizations to consider their example.

Doug and I made an appointment with our pastor to discuss the messages from fellow parishioners. Before the meeting I was in tears.

"Doug, it hurts so much to feel despised in my own church, and this time, for doing what I know God called me to do! Every week since we came here, the words of the confession worked their way into my heart—calling me to confess my sin and leave it behind.

Finally I did, and now I no longer feel welcome to come. It's all so backward and wrong."

Clearly the conversation was difficult for our pastor as well. When, in the end, we decided that it was too painful to stay, the pastor made an interesting comment.

"I don't think you realize how much your spiritual life has been shaped by this church," he said. I understood him to mean that we should recognize the wisdom of the church's pro-choice stance.

"Oh, I do realize it," I said. For I knew that God had met me there, had called to me directly, not through the agenda of the church, but through the power of the Spirit, as I had prayed, week after week, these words from *The Book of Common Prayer.* May we all pray these words, and live them.

Most merciful God,
we confess that we have sinned against you
in thought, word, and deed,
by what we have done,
and by what we have left undone.
We have not loved you with our whole heart;
we have not loved our neighbors as ourselves.
We are truly sorry and we humbly repent.
For the sake of your Son Jesus Christ,
have mercy on us and forgive us;
that we may delight in your will,
and walk in your ways,
to the glory of your Name. Amen.[16]

CHAPTER TWENTY-ONE

The Unexpected Gift

AMONG THE MEDIA INQUIRIES we received in those first few days was a big, scary one—an invitation to appear on *The O'Reilly Factor.* And what made it even more scary than the idea of appearing on such a widely viewed show was the tentative date they'd given us for my appearance—just before the hearing on the preliminary injunction from Planned Parenthood. Would I say something that would jeopardize our case? Would I give Planned Parenthood ammunition to use against me in court?

It didn't take long to figure out that, if I was going to appear, I'd have to appear with Jeff Paradowski, my attorney, so that if Bill O'Reilly asked me something I shouldn't answer, Jeff would be there to stop me.

So Shawn called Jeff to ask if he'd be willing to appear on the show with me, and he immediately answered yes. Later, though, he admitted, "To be honest with you, I was very nervous about it. This wasn't just some local station. This was national. So I called Shawn and said, 'I want to do it, but we'd better make sure we're ready. We need to prepare for this.'"

Jeff and I met with Jeff Blaszak, a local cable company director who does a lot of multimedia work for the Coalition for Life. He ran us through a mock interview, firing questions at us as if he were Bill O'Reilly. After we'd done that three or four times, we felt ready.

But it wasn't to be—at least not yet. On November 5, 2009, a gunman shot and killed twelve people and wounded another thirty-one at Fort Hood, Texas. Suddenly O'Reilly and others had something much more tragic and newsworthy to cover, and my appearance with Bill O'Reilly was postponed until November 11. Since the hearing was over by then, there was no need for Jeff Paradowski to appear with me to keep me from saying something that would hurt our case—but Shawn went on with me.

But our little story in Bryan, Texas, continued to attract significant media attention. Most of it seemed to come from the Christian media—magazines and radio and TV programs. But occasionally we'd be contacted by someone I thought might slant the article in a way that would distort my perspective. I was contacted, for instance, by a reporter from Salon.com, which describes itself as an "online arts and culture magazine" but is often criticized for its left-leaning viewpoint. I almost didn't call the reporter back, but in the end I decided to do it. Their article wasn't as bad as I'd feared. At the end, she called me the "next right-wing media darling."[17] And I thought, *I've been called much worse. If that's the worst she can come up with, I'm okay.* The bloggers continued to slam me from all directions, and through it I was learning the valuable lesson of trusting God and God alone for my reputation.

I was also contacted by ABCNews.com. I did a telephone

interview with them that appeared in an article on their Web site. It was actually very good—fair and complete.[18]

I had initially been pretty circumspect on my Facebook page—I mentioned that I was leaving Planned Parenthood, but not why, and I mentioned nothing at first about the Coalition for Life. But as the story came out, I started getting around 150 messages a day on my Facebook page—all of them supportive. I didn't receive one negative message.

On Friday, November 6, I flew to New York to appear on *Huckabee* on Fox News. I had talked the day before to Wes Yoder, who runs the Ambassador Speakers Bureau and handles all of Shawn's appearances. The advice Wes gave me about the interview with Mike Huckabee was, "Just be you. Tell your story. You don't need talking points—this is just about being honest and genuine." He was so right! How freeing to no longer be bound to the Planned Parenthood official talking points I'd had for so many years.

I flew out by myself; Doug stayed home, pulling babysitting duty with Grace but also showing up at work—after all, Doug's salary was the only income we had at this point.

Sadly, the repercussions of speaking out took a further toll on some friendships. My friend Valerie had been, for a long time, my trusted right hand at the clinic. She'd left when she received a promotion to another clinic—but unfortunately that hadn't worked out. A few months before I left Planned Parenthood, she'd left the organization and for a short time after that, she and her child had lived with Doug and me while she got back on her feet.

Valerie and I had now been very close for years. I wasn't worried about losing my friendship with her. The thought of it had never occurred to me. Our friendship was too close for that. Or so I thought.

I hadn't talked to her for several days. I'd texted her a couple of times and hadn't heard anything back. But I didn't think much of it. *It happens,* I told myself. *People get busy. She's probably scolding herself right now for not getting back to me.*

A few days after *Huckabee,* Doug said, "Have you heard anything from Valerie lately?"

"No," I said. "I was just thinking about calling her."

"Well, if you do, maybe you can clear up something strange. I was on Facebook today, and I noticed that apparently I've been removed from Valerie's friends list."

My heart sank. As soon as I could, I went onto Facebook myself, and sure enough, I'd been removed from Valerie's friends list too. Since then, no communication whatsoever. Another close friendship bit the dust.

But the process of seeing previously close friends turn away from me because we now disagreed about the crucial issue of abortion reminds me of the very different brand of friendship I'm also seeing in action these days. I'm thinking of people like Elizabeth, Marilisa, some friends from church and even college days—people who befriended me and stood by me for years *even though they did not agree with what I did at Planned Parenthood, even though they do not believe in abortion.* Those people modeled for me something far deeper, far stronger than situational friendship: they loved and accepted me even when I was (or am) doing something they found morally objectionable. They didn't just talk about love—they put flesh on that concept.

Many of those people are contacting me now, telling me how proud they are of me and how much they love me. That means a great deal to me—because of one thing. I know they loved me *then,* too.

One other thing happened about this time that reminded me that, while I was losing some things by the stand I was taking, I was gaining much more. My first husband, Mark, and I had divorced in 2003, and I had not seen his son, Justin, since then. Not that I hadn't thought about him. I loved Justin as if he'd been my own birth son. For the two years Mark and I were married, Justin had called me his "other mom," and we'd been as close as any other parent and child. To lose him through divorce was unbelievably hard, and I had grieved that loss ever since.

After one of my appearances on Fox, I got a Facebook message from Justin. He was now thirteen—and I'd had no contact with him since he was seven. The subject line on his message said, "Hey, miss me?"

His note began, "Hey, it's me, Justin, from a long time ago." At first, I couldn't even read the rest. I read that far and just began to weep—from happiness that I was hearing from him again after so long, when I'd had no real hope of ever hearing from him again; from sorrow that we'd lost so much time together. Here he was, now thirteen, a young man. He'd been just a little boy when I'd seen him last.

I wrote back as soon as I had my emotions under control and said, "Oh, Justin—I think about you every day. And I have since the last time I saw you."

Justin's grandmother, Mark's ex-mother-in-law, with whom I'd always had a really good relationship, also wrote me that night. She told me how proud she was of me for taking this stand. They'd seen me on TV that day, and it made them want to reach out to me. So they found me on Facebook. She told me that when Justin had received my response, telling him that I still thought about him every day, he got very emotional.

I wish he lived closer—Justin and his family live halfway across the country from me. But we now keep in touch by e-mail and have become close again. I hope to reconnect face-to-face one day. And as with so many other things, it would never have happened if I hadn't been forced to face what I was engaged in at that clinic in Bryan, Texas—and if Planned Parenthood hadn't decided to make it a public spectacle.

I was beginning to discover that when we set our feet upon the red carpet that God rolls out before us, He surprises us with unexpected delights. The joy of my reconnection with Justin—the son of my heart whom I thought I'd forever lost—gave me the lift I needed to face my fear of the uncertain future.

CHAPTER TWENTY-TWO

The Hearing

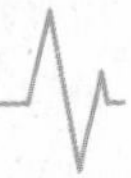

SHAWN TOLD ME LATER that when he left his house on the morning of November 10, the day of the hearing, Marilisa was nervous. "Don't worry, babe," he said, leaning down to kiss her. "It's going to be fun."

"Fun?" she asked skeptically.

"Sure," he said, "and besides, I promise to use my one phone call to call you."

Despite her nervousness, he managed to get a laugh out of her. And that reflects something for which I feel extremely fortunate. The same instinct that made him protect Marilisa from the tension of the court date by joking with her about it made him protect me. Between Shawn and Jeff, I must say that even if I didn't always feel like it at the time, I was well protected. Not just from the injunction itself, or the tension of awaiting the hearing, but even from the intense preparation of the defense. I didn't even have to ask myself, *How will I find a lawyer?* I was protected from all of that because

Shawn and Jeff knew I wouldn't be able, at that difficult point—having been betrayed by friends and threatened with legal action in the midst of wrenching personal changes both in vocation and in my entire value system—to maneuver through that minefield. So they negotiated it for me.

Even though Shawn was trying to set everyone else at ease, he was nervous. He, Doug, and I had agreed to meet at Jeff's office so the four of us could drive to the courthouse together for the hearing. He wanted to get to Jeff's office before me, and he did—by about forty-five minutes! And when he arrived, Jeff—who will be late to his own funeral—was already there, dressed for court. "How do you feel?" Shawn asked him.

"Good," Jeff said. "I feel good."

Right, Shawn thought. Five minutes later, he asked again.

"Uh, pretty nervous," Jeff admitted this time.

Jeff was *nervous*? Jeff, who has won some pretty impressive cases against massive firms and their brilliant attorneys, Jeff who has sued the state of Texas, Jeff who exudes confidence—he was nervous about *my* case?

But by the time Doug and I arrived, any signs of that nervousness, for either of them, had disappeared, and they looked cool as could be. We got into Jeff's car and headed to the courthouse—each of us looking pretty impressive, I must say, in our suits. We were all nervous, but none of us admitted it, trying as hard as we could to set the others at ease. Shawn and Jeff, as usual, laughed all the way.

We pulled up in front of the courthouse, and Jeff said, quietly, "My mom's going to be here." I was struck by the significance of this case to Jeff and his family. My lawyer's mom was going to be here for my hearing. "There she is," he said, pointing.

I couldn't believe the timing as I said, "My mom's here too. Look, there she is."

And Shawn laughed and said, "Okay, the gang's all here. Now let's go beat this thing!" And then he grabbed my arm and whimpered, "Mom—hold my hand!" We all just lost it—total crack-up. Here we were, about to go in to face Planned Parenthood in a hearing we couldn't afford to lose, scared out of our wits, and we were laughing like loons in front of the courthouse.

Some of this was probably just our way of releasing tension. Shawn and Jeff had been spending countless hours preparing for this hearing, trying to anticipate everything that might come up and then making sure they were prepared for it—even though most of it probably *wouldn't* come up. "It was like preparing for a research paper that you'll never write," Shawn said later.

For Shawn, it was in many ways like a perfect storm of stress. Not only was there the legal stress of the hearing, he was traveling and speaking a lot. *And* he had just found out that the following summer he'd be uprooting his family to move to Virginia to work full-time on coordinating a national 40 Days for Life campaign. None of us had any idea how much stress he was under.

My mom and a friend of hers were walking toward us.

"Oh, you've got to meet my mom." I was excited. In all the years I'd been with Planned Parenthood, my mom had never met a single person I'd worked with, and that had been more than fine with me. In contrast, I found myself wonderfully excited to connect Mom with the Coalition for Life people. Shawn told me later that he was nervous about meeting her. He had envisioned that my family—and my friends, for that matter—were probably all militantly pro-choice. So imagine his surprise and relief when my mom came walking up to him, face glowing, threw her arms around him, kissed him on the cheek, and said, "Thank you for getting her out of there."

Unified, bound in spirit, we headed inside, Doug clasping my hand tightly. Other than our moms, we weren't expecting much of a crowd. In fact, we'd sent an e-mail to our Coalition for Life supporters and staff asking them *not* to attend. Jeff knew enough about this judge, J. D. Langley, to know that having four hundred Coalition supporters on the sidewalks, holding up signs and chanting "Free Abby!" wouldn't exactly endear us to him. And he'd banned cameras from the hearing—the media could attend, and did, but no cameras were allowed. So we knew the number of people in the courtroom would be small, and that was fine with us.

It was all very awkward, of course. The people I was facing in this hearing, the plaintiffs, were all people I'd worked with daily until a month before, people I considered friends. But their attitude now was anything but friendly. Walking into the courtroom, I found myself entering side by side with a Planned Parenthood board member and his wife. The board member's expression seemed closed and cold, as if he felt I'd gone over to the enemy, and I understood that from his perspective, I had. He looked at me once and then just turned away.

Most of the Planned Parenthood people were already there when we entered. We'd subpoenaed Megan, Taylor, another staff member, and one of the abortion doctors (I'll call him Dr. A). Along with the board member, Cheryl and several others from Planned Parenthood were there, including Planned Parenthood's New York PR team.

Dr. A's presence there had a power and influence all its own. He was there at *our* request—we'd subpoenaed him. The reason we wanted him there was to establish that his identity was not a secret, as Planned Parenthood alleged in their petition. They said that my knowledge of his identity was a threat to him and to their operation. But his presence there was a production. The courthouse had called Jeff ahead of time to let us know they would be bringing him in secretly through a back entrance. He was represented by an attorney of his own, and he even had a security detail—courtesy of the National Abortion Federation, all the way from D.C. It seemed, on one hand, completely unnecessary to provide that kind of security to protect Dr. A from a peace-loving organization like Coalition for Life. But it's also true that it had been less than six months since Dr. George Tiller, the soft-spoken abortionist much vilified by antiabortionist groups, had been gunned down during a Sunday morning service at his church. The memory of that was fresh in everyone's mind.

The courtroom setup resembled the typical courtroom I'd seen on TV, though it was smaller than I'd imagined. The judge's bench was front and center with a witness stand to the right of it. Planned Parenthood and their legal team of two, along with the abortion doctor's lawyer, sat at a long table on the right as we faced the bench, and we took our places at the table on the left. The room was surprisingly plain and worn, our table scratched from years of use.

Sitting behind us on our side was a select handful of supporters. Besides Doug, our moms, and just a few friends, there were some visiting pro-life attorneys. Though not handling our case, they had expressed their willingness to help us out later if necessary, depending on how the hearing went.

Jeff was still laughing and joking as we entered, trying to keep things light, maybe for his own sake as well as ours. But as Shawn and I took our seats, Jeff strode confidently to the two attorneys for Planned Parenthood and courteously introduced himself. A few moments later they followed suit, coming over to our side. Shadow Sloan, a tall, red-headed woman I knew from a number of meetings, and her cocounsel, Deborah Milner, introduced themselves to Shawn courteously. They'd ignored me up to this point, but then Shadow smiled tersely at me. "Hi, Abby," she said.

"Hi, Shadow—how are you?" I said. I hated the awkwardness of it. It hurt that other than Shadow and Deborah, none of the others made any effort to greet me or even nod in my direction. I'm sure they'd been told not to, but still, these were longtime friends and former coworkers. I looked at Megan and Taylor. I couldn't believe that, as much as we'd gone through together, especially in those final days at Planned Parenthood, they wouldn't even look my way. I was trying to imagine what they could possibly say at this hearing, given the accusations in the court papers. Surely they weren't going to take the stand and actually testify against me, were they? How could they? Why would they? They were my friends.

After the two attorneys went back to their side of the room, Jeff continued with his clever comments to ease my tension, and I was glad he was doing it, but a storm of thoughts kept running through my mind. I was worried, obviously, about how this would turn out—what the judge would decide. But I knew, at least, that the burden of proof didn't lie with us. Jeff had assured me that, since Planned Parenthood had filed the petition, the burden of proof rested with them to prove that I had done something wrong, to prove that I was a threat to them, and he was convinced that they didn't have a case. I just hoped he was right.

One thing gave me real confidence: Jeff was a seasoned trial lawyer, and he'd handled some big cases. The Planned Parenthood team had far less courtroom experience than Jeff. But they certainly must have prepared for this within an inch of their lives because they had brought *boxes and boxes* of material—they were surrounded by the boxes of what I imagined must have been supporting material, if they needed it. Either that or they were moving out of their apartment. Jeff wasn't impressed, though. "Just pomp," he told me later. "Trying to intimidate us. It didn't work." Well, maybe it didn't work on him.

I didn't know whether I'd get up on the stand or not that morning. Jeff was prepared to call me if needed, though he seemed confident it wouldn't come to that. And in one way, I *wanted* to be called—I wanted to tell my story in my own words. I hoped I would get that chance. I was fired up! But more than that, I wanted to hear what Planned Parenthood had to say. What on earth was their case going to be? I couldn't imagine.

I looked at Taylor and Megan and Cheryl and my stomach did flip-flops. I knew they would put those three on the stand, and I was ready—ready to face them, to hear their testimony with my own ears. But on the other hand, I was nervous about what they would say. How would it feel to hear a friend contradict what I knew to be true?

Mostly, though, I was pumped. Feeling up to the challenge. Yes, I'd initially felt bewildered and hurt by Megan and Taylor's statements, but now the adrenaline was flowing. I was ready for them to say directly to my face what they'd said in the petition. I knew I was telling the truth and so had nothing to worry about.

Both Jeff and I had a nagging fear, though, that Planned Parenthood had something up its sleeve—some bomb to drop into the hearing that we hadn't anticipated. They were supposed to have revealed everything to us, of course, but we've all watched enough courtroom dramas to know there can be last-minute surprises. We simply kept wondering, given how weak their case appeared to be, if there could be something of which we were unaware that made them willing to take this case to the courtroom.

Everyone rose; the judge entered and asked us all to be seated. The attorneys introduced themselves, including Dr. A's attorney. The plaintiffs, Planned Parenthood, got the opportunity to present their case first, since the burden of proof lay with them. If they couldn't prove their case, then there *was* no case, and that's what Jeff was hoping for. Early on, Jeff wisely requested that the judge have all witnesses removed from the courtroom so they could not hear one another's testimony. The judge agreed.

Shadow Sloan called Cheryl to the stand first.

Starting with Cheryl was, I suspected, not going to be a good strategy for Planned Parenthood. In my opinion, Cheryl tended to be ill at ease in front of groups of people, so I didn't think she'd be a convincing or eloquent witness. I believe I was right.

After Cheryl testified that Planned Parenthood had confidential information, Shadow asked, "Can you describe, please, what that confidential information consists of?"[19]

"Patient records, which we protect at all costs," Cheryl said, "HR personnel records, our security procedures, and our policies and procedures regarding how we operate in the clinic."

"Now, ma'am, you told us about confidential information regarding patients, staff, and service providers. Is the identity of the service providers also subject to confidentiality at Planned Parenthood?"

"Yes, it is."

"Why is that, please?"

"Because we're concerned for our providers' safety and we don't want anything to happen to them."

This, of course, was a crucial issue: did I possess knowledge that, if I decided to divulge it, would endanger the lives of Planned Parenthood's "service providers"—in other words, the abortion doctors?

Shadow questioned Cheryl about these records at some length—was this information known outside Planned Parenthood, was it known by all employees, would Abby Johnson have had access to this information, and so on. Then she concluded her questioning of Cheryl, and Jeff began his cross-examination.

"You've identified information that you and counsel claim to be confidential. Let's start with the patient records. Specifically I presume you're talking about patients who come to the Bryan clinic for services, be they family planning, contraception, or abortion services; is that correct?"

"Yes."

"And these would be their client files and patient records pertaining to the treatment that they received; right?"

"Right."

Throughout her testimony, Cheryl kept her eyes on the attorneys. She didn't look my way once.

"What evidence do you have that Abby Johnson took some of this patient record information?"

"I don't have firsthand knowledge."

"I'm sorry?"

"I don't have firsthand knowledge. I was not there that day."

"You don't have any evidence or proof to give to Judge Langley today that Ms. Johnson took any of these patient records?"

"I do not personally have that."

And so it went for the next several minutes. Jeff would mention each type of information that Planned Parenthood claimed I possessed that they considered confidential and ask Cheryl whether she had firsthand information that I had taken any such information off the premises of the Bryan clinic. Again and again, Cheryl was forced to answer that she did not.

It didn't take Jeff long to get to the question of the identity of the doctor we had subpoenaed, who was of course sitting there in the courtroom with us. Everyone was careful not to mention his name, however. We felt we had a strong case here—Planned Parenthood was trying so hard to make it appear that the identity of those doctors who perform abortions for them is a big secret, and to tell the truth, some of the doctors did go to some lengths to obscure their identity, having themselves driven to the clinic by chauffeurs rather than driving their own cars, walking from car to clinic with a sheet over their heads, and so on. Some, but not all. Dr. A had been interviewed about abortions in the media. So if he was willing to "out" himself, how could my knowledge of what he did be a threat? Anyone who'd seen him interviewed on TV knew what he did for a living.

But for now, Jeff simply established through his questioning of Cheryl that all of that information concerning the doctors—which doctors served the clinic, which days they came, where they were picked up, and so on—changed on a regular basis, so any knowledge I had would be outdated and inaccurate.

Cheryl was dismissed, and Planned Parenthood called Taylor to the stand.

Poor Taylor—still a teenager and caught in such an ugly conflict. I was upset that she had to testify, and I felt sorry for her. I'd always felt protective of her, and today was no exception. As she came into the room, I could see how anxious she was. Bewildered by what the preliminary injunction had said, I watched her closely, trying to understand what could have happened between her late-night sessions at my home, when I'd helped her write her résumé and apply for jobs, and the day she'd disconnected her cell phone and allowed Planned Parenthood to cite falsehoods of those events in their petition and temporary restraining order.

From the beginning she had a hard time controlling her emotions. When she took the stand, she looked at me, and that, I believe, was her undoing. She looked right at me as she spoke; her voice trembled, and tears rolled down her face. It was heart-wrenching, and I found my anger building—not at her, but at Planned Parenthood for whatever they might have said or done to set her up for this. Her testimony took a very long time because she often had to work to get herself under control before she could answer the questions.

It seemed Deborah Milner's questioning of Taylor was intended to establish that I had tried to influence Taylor to leave Planned Parenthood, that I had manipulated her résumé and employment applications without her permission, and that I had given her records relating to her employment that she was not supposed to have had, records that were kept locked up. This, of course, was not the way it had happened.

Taylor was struggling enough when Deborah was questioning her, but it became even harder for her when Jeff began his cross-examination, perhaps because his voice and tone with her were so gentle. I could see that Jeff intuitively understood that Taylor was as much a victim in all of this as I was. Sometimes she would be crying so hard that she couldn't catch her breath. Still, he had to establish the contradiction between what she was saying now and what the court papers stated she'd said.

"You and Abby Johnson are friends, are you not?" Jeff asked.

"Yes." Her eyes were on mine.

"At one time you wanted to leave [the] Planned Parenthood clinic and find another job—"

"All of the staff were confused after she left. We weren't sure if we wanted to stay or not."

"Okay."

"We were being told different things."

Her voice was shaking, and tears rolled down her cheeks.

"Okay," Jeff continued. "You wanted to leave Planned Parenthood because it was causing you a moral conflict, wasn't it?"

"No."

Jeff then introduced as evidence Taylor's recent employment application. "Do you recognize that employment application?" he asked.

"Yes," Taylor said.

"That's your handwriting, isn't it?"

"Yes."

"And this is an application for employment that you filled out over at Abby Johnson's house; right?"

"Yes. This is the application that she gave me and the—under where it says reason for leaving, she had told me to write that."

"Okay. You were wanting to have Abby help you find another job; right?"

"She offered to help other staff find other jobs also."

"Okay." Jeff sensed her fear and tried to probe its cause. "Are you scared about your employment there at Planned Parenthood, Taylor?"

"No."

"Okay. I just want to make sure you don't have any fear that if you leave Planned Parenthood the same thing that's happened to Abby Johnson—this whole procedure and everything might happen to you."

"No." Her eyes were on mine, and I am sure she saw my own sadness, my disapproval, my pain. More tears rolled down her face.

"Okay. That hadn't crossed your mind? You have no fear about that?"

"No."

"Okay. You haven't asked yourself, 'How will I pay for an attorney?' or anything like that?"

"No."

Jeff and Shawn and I had discussed the possibility that, since Planned Parenthood didn't really have a very strong case here, they may have initiated this action for some other reason than expecting to win it. Such as sending a message to other employees, like Taylor. Or putting Coalition for Life on the defensive and warning them off. But if Taylor *was* afraid that Planned Parenthood might come after her, she'd be unlikely to admit that with them sitting right there, oath or not. So Jeff moved on.

"You filled out this application over at Abby Johnson's house?"

"Yes."

"On page 2 it says, 'reason for leaving Planned Parenthood'—correct me if I'm wrong, but you wrote—this is your writing, 'I feel I can no longer work at this job due to moral conflict.'"

"Correct. She had told me to write that."

After questioning Taylor about how much influence I could have had over her, considering that I was no longer her supervisor, he said, "Now, you say that Abby Johnson prepared your résumé."

"Yes."

"But you helped her prepare the résumé on Abby's computer at her house?"

"No. She typed it up at her house."

"Okay. She—"

"I was at my house when she was typing it."

"Okay. And you were giving her the information over the phone on what to type?"

"The only information I gave was my employment at my grandparents'."

I couldn't believe it. I looked at Doug, and he just looked back at me while shaking his head. Taylor and I had stayed up until late into the night at my house working on that résumé—at her request! And now she was testifying, under oath, that she hadn't even been there, that it had all been my idea? I had a pen in hand at the time and, without realizing it, was furiously clicking it open and closed. Shawn gently reached over and took it from me, and the sudden silence made me realize that the sound must have been echoing in the courtroom, and I had no idea for how long. I shrank down in my seat.

All in all, I thought Jeff's handling of Taylor was gentle and kind. He told me later that he felt like she was just in a hurry to get it done and get out of here, and he thought, *If I let her do that, we'll get done that much sooner.* He noted that she was shaking—looking at Cheryl, clearly afraid of something, and looking back at me tearfully. Despite what she said, he thought she was afraid for her job, and afraid this—the courtroom unpleasantness—could happen to her if she resigned. He didn't think her testimony would do us much harm. And frankly, he wanted her to know that, if she ever did decide to leave Planned Parenthood, she would be treated kindly by the Coalition for Life.

Jeff continued to question her about the employment application, about the résumé and the resignation letter, about who typed what where, about whether she had been looking for another job—"No," she said—and about what she claimed to have seen me printing out at Planned Parenthood that last day. It was lengthy testimony, made longer by her sobbing, and when Jeff concluded his cross-examination, she was allowed to leave the stand before Deborah's redirect so she could collect herself.

As she stepped down, my heart was torn in two. On the one hand, I was so angry. I wanted to question her myself, to set the record straight. I knew that after a few words from me she'd break and tell the truth, and I was itching to have at it. But just as powerful was my feeling of deep sympathy for her. She looked, as she slumped her way out of the courtroom, like a whipped dog, beaten and wounded. I remembered her excitement at dinner just a few days before, talking about her future, nursing school, providing health care far away from abortion. I wanted the best for Taylor, and now I saw her as yet another victim of Planned Parenthood. I looked across the room at their board member and legal team, the supposed protectors of women in crisis. But they weren't even watching her, as if she were invisible to them.

And I suspect she was.

CHAPTER TWENTY-THREE

The Ruling

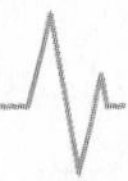

Deborah Milner called Megan to the stand.

The door at the back of the courtroom opened, and Megan *marched* to the front of the courtroom. Her demeanor was very different from Taylor's. Whereas Taylor was very tearful the whole time, Megan seemed angry and, like Cheryl, did not look at me at all. Her manner was terse and her answers short, delivered in a clipped tone. She looked disgusted.

As the testimony went on, I was struck by the absurdity of the entire scenario. We were sitting in a court of law, using the valuable resources of our judicial system, two legal teams, even a security detail for the abortion doctor. Media reporters were taking notes, and outside cameras were waiting. We were all listening to testimony about, of all things, simple job descriptions and résumés that my friends had asked my help on—help I'd gladly given.

I thought back on the frightening words in the temporary

restraining order: *Plaintiffs are entitled to a temporary restraining order because there is evidence that harm is imminent to Plaintiffs, and if the Court does not issue the temporary restraining order, Plaintiffs will be irreparably harmed by the disclosure of confidential information.*

This was a circus, and I was angry.

Jeff's line of questioning with Megan validated my feelings.

"Now, you don't hide the fact from anybody that you are a nurse-practitioner at Planned Parenthood, do you?" Jeff asked.

"No."

"In fact, you've got a MySpace page which I can pull up—or anyone can pull up. And on there you state 'Planned Parenthood of Houston and Southeast Texas, Bryan, Texas, nurse-practitioner'?"

"Yes."

"You asked Abby Johnson, 'Where can I find my job description,' she found it for you, printed it off, and gave it to you so that you could update your résumé, right?"

"Yes. Uh-huh."

After verifying with her that there was nothing secret or confidential about the job description, he asked, "At one time you and Abby Johnson and Taylor were all planning to leave your employment at Planned Parenthood; isn't that right?"

I looked directly at her face, holding my breath for her response.

"Yes."

"And you updated your résumé, you e-mailed it to Abby Johnson—"

"Yes."

"—and said, 'Here you go. Good luck to me'?"

"Uh-huh."

"Right?" Jeff asked again, driving the point home for the court.

"Yes."

Whew! She admitted that she was the one who mailed it to me, not that I'd taken it without her permission!

Jeff pressed forward. "Abby Johnson went through with it and left her employment; you changed your mind and decided to stay?"

"Yes."

"And that's as simple as it is, correct?"

"Yes."

It felt good to hear those words. For the most part, her testimony covered about the same ground as Cheryl's and Taylor's, except for one thing.

One night after I'd left Planned Parenthood, a friend had come by whose pierced ear had become infected. I wanted to help her, but her ear was so painful and tender that everything I did hurt her. I called Megan and asked if she had any lidocaine cream at home.

"No," she said. "I have some at the clinic, but I don't have the new security code there." They'd changed all the codes after I resigned.

"That's okay," I said. "I can use something else." And that was the end of it.

But in Megan's testimony, it sounded completely different. She made it sound as if I'd been after not the lidocaine but the security code. Planned Parenthood was clearly hoping that my phone call to Megan that night would incriminate me in some way, or at least reflect poorly on me. But in his cross-examination, Jeff dismissed these concerns pretty easily, pointing out that lidocaine is commonly available and is not an industrial secret for Planned Parenthood. Furthermore, even if the security code for the clinic had been compromised, it could have been immediately changed, as they already had done after I resigned. The whole subject was silly, of course. I hadn't even asked Megan for the code, merely asked if she had some lidocaine cream.

One thing in Jeff's cross-examination of Megan hurt. When he asked if she was a friend of mine, she answered, "Until recently, yes." And I thought, *When did that change? And how? What did I do?* I still don't understand that.

After a brief redirect and cross-examination of Taylor, once she'd regained control of her emotions, Planned Parenthood concluded its case. We had, of course, prepared a case of our own in defense, but Jeff had another tactic to try first.

Judge Langley asked Jeff, "Are you planning on putting on any testimony?"

"Well, Your Honor," Jeff replied, "it depends. I'd like to move at this time for a directed verdict and a request that the temporary injunction be denied; and if you would hear me for a minute, Judge, I'll give you the reasons for my request."

Jeff went on to argue that none of their three witnesses had offered any evidence that I had taken any confidential information from Planned Parenthood. In any event, the material Planned Parenthood described as confidential was not, in fact, confidential at all, as for instance the formula for Coca-Cola would be. All of it was readily available elsewhere or, as in the case of the building security code, could easily be changed.

"On that basis, Judge, I would ask . . . that their request be denied and that the temporary restraining order be dissolved."

Deborah Milner offered a response on the part of Planned Parenthood, but it didn't alter the basic truths of Jeff's argument.

Judge Langley's response: "I don't find enough information here to indicate that Ms. Johnson has broken her agreement. Temporary injunction denied. Temporary restraining order dissolved immediately. We're adjourned."

We had won.

As soon as the judge announced his decision, Shawn and I jumped up and hugged. Then there were hugs all around. Someone yelled, "Yes!" and I laughed.

About an hour and a half. That's how long the whole thing had taken. After all that anxiety, all that concern about how things might end up—an hour and a half, and now it was done. I stood there, watching what was happening around me. That was it? We were done? Had I misunderstood what the judge had said?

This was what we had hoped for, of course—that the judge would deny the preliminary injunction—but I felt a twinge of a letdown and realized how much I'd wanted to get up on the stand, tell what I knew to be true, and defend myself! I had wanted to set the record straight.

But God knew what He was doing by not giving me that opportunity. And by this point in my new journey of trusting God, I understood. I was so fired up, I'm afraid I'd have gone on the attack. I would probably have said something that I would have regretted later. I'm hoping—praying—that my relationship with some of those friends and coworkers can be repaired and reestablished at some point. If I'd testified that day, I might have unintentionally closed those doors.

Jeff gathered up his papers and packed them away. "I feel like we just won the Super Bowl," Shawn said, still grinning. I did too—and I didn't.

I watched the Planned Parenthood team—their lawyers, their

New York PR team, the abortion doctor's lawyer, the board member and his wife. They moved quickly to pack everything away, and then they began shuffling out through a side door. Clearly they had no desire to speak to me or the media. In fact, they looked as if they were in shock. I didn't see an angry face among them. It was more as if they couldn't fathom what had just happened. I thought about how much I'd loved this organization, how I'd wanted to serve and please them. Now they looked like a sad and sorry lot to me.

Shawn watched them file out. "Well," he said, "the truth won out!"

We pushed open the courtroom doors to head out and I couldn't believe it. Journalists and broadcasters who'd sat through the hearing had gathered—now *with* their cameras. Immediately there were microphones in my face. Cameras flashed, reporters were vying for position to get close to me, asking me questions. As director of a Planned Parenthood clinic, I was no stranger to the media or to having to make public statements. But this felt completely different. I felt like I'd fallen into some made-for-TV movie. It seemed surreal.

"Ms. Johnson," one reporter said, "now that the gag order has been lifted, what do you have to say? What can you tell us that you weren't able to before?"

And it was the strangest thing. How could I explain that my story was still exactly the same? I had already told the story of the ultrasound-guided abortion on the local news, of my sudden desperate conviction that I had believed a lie, and that I had to now reject that lie and follow the truth, which meant leaving Planned Parenthood and, instead, working on behalf of women *and* the unborn. All of that I had already said—it was my story, just my story, and that's all I had to say from the first, and it's all I had to say the day of the hearing.

And suddenly the utter ridiculousness of what Planned Parenthood had done with their restraining order hit home. They had tried to keep me from saying—what, exactly? All I wanted to do was tell my own story, the story of my own change of heart, and they had never been able to stop me from doing that. For the rest of it—never in a million years would I have even considered violating the privacy of the clinic's patients by releasing information about them. I still care about those women and families. Not past tense—I didn't care about them only when I worked at Planned Parenthood. Present tense: I cared about them the morning of the hearing, and I still care about them now. And in a way, I care even more now that I understand all the more the deep harm abortion does to a woman. I wouldn't have released private information about them when I worked at the clinic, and I won't do it now.

All of this media attention, the microphones in front of my face that morning, the reporters asking me to tell them my story—none of that had come about because I had asked for it. It had come about because Planned Parenthood had filed for an injunction, supposedly to keep me quiet, but instead it meant that thousands would hear me talk about the work that God had done in my heart on a day when I hadn't asked for it, hadn't expected it, and frankly, hadn't wanted it—on a day when a doctor had needed someone to hold an ultrasound wand. If they didn't like what I was saying, if they don't like that you're reading these words now in this book—well, in my view, they've done it to themselves. None of it would have happened if not for the media storm they unleashed with their petition and their press release to publicize it.

Planned Parenthood made no statement to the press immediately after the hearing, but they did release a statement picked up in our local paper: "Today's judgment is a blow to medical privacy and client confidentiality."[20]

I knew only too well the tactics their words demonstrated; tactics I myself had been taught to use—word choices that gave the impression that Coalition for Life was a threat to the safety of patients and clinic workers. The irony of their claim struck me. I'd just seen what they had done to my own friends in the courtroom, their own clinic workers. And I knew of the boardroom conversations and mandates to increase the number of abortions to increase their revenue. As a result, I agreed that there *was* a threat to the safety of patients and clinic workers—but in my opinion that threat came from within Planned Parenthood itself. I was now part of the movement to truly protect patients and clinic workers, and I'd be doing so from the right side of the fence.

There was still the small matter of the lawsuit Planned Parenthood had filed against me, saying I'd violated my employment contract by breaking the confidentiality agreement with patients. Jeff wasn't worried. He sent them a letter the day after the hearing, saying that in light of the way the hearing had turned out, they had no chance of prevailing in the lawsuit. If they didn't drop it, he added, he would ask the court to have Planned Parenthood pay all of my attorney fees. The lawsuit was officially dropped on November 17. And believe it or not, that's the last thing I've heard from Planned Parenthood. No more legal action, and in fact no more communication at their initiation of any kind. I occasionally see some of my former colleagues, however, as I stand and pray at the fence outside the clinic. I still care about them and pray for them daily, and I know from my own story that the answer to prayer can take a very long time.

Shawn told me later that after Doug and I headed out to lunch with my mom, he took Jeff for a victory lunch at a grungy place in downtown Bryan. Jeff had pulled his tie loose and unbuttoned his collar by that time, and the two of them just sat, staring at each other and saying nothing, emotionally exhausted. A waitress came and took their order, then brought their drinks.

Shawn took a sip. "Jeff, my friend, I know better than anybody how hard you worked on all this. And you know what? Right now you look as tapped out as I feel. I got nothing left, man."

Jeff nodded. "My exhaustion is exceeded only by my excitement that we won."

"There's a problem," Shawn said.

Jeff cocked an eyebrow. "How can there be a problem?"

"The problem is, you've given this so much, and there isn't any way we can repay you. You won't make a penny off this. And that's not fair. How many other cases do you have going on right now?"

Jeff chuckled. "Sixty-seven."

Shawn shook his head. "Sixty-seven other cases, and you gave us all your time? Listen, I can go to some of our donors, see if I can shake loose some money to cover some of your time. . . ."

Jeff said, "No, don't bother. Truth is, I've missed so many of my stand-and-pray hours at the clinic—maybe this makes up for it. Can we just be even?"

Shawn laughed. "Tell you what. I'll pay for lunch."

Lunch cost $17.50.

Shawn walked out of the restaurant thinking, *We got a pretty good return on our investment for that lunch.*

CHAPTER TWENTY-FOUR

The Revelation

I STILL GET GOOSE BUMPS when I think about the things you're about to read in this chapter. It was when I became aware of them that I fully realized how everything I've gone through has been part of a much larger picture—that my story is just a small part of something God has been doing since long before I showed up at the volunteer fair at Texas A&M. And I trust it will go on long after I've played my part.

When I stumbled, weeping, through the back door of our Coalition for Life office that fifth day in October 2009, I had no idea that our two organizations, Planned Parenthood and Coalition for Life, had much more linking them than the fact that Abby Johnson was groping her way blindly from one to the other.

The Bryan, Texas, Planned Parenthood clinic first opened in 1975. Then in 1998 they announced a move to a new facility in Bryan that, beginning in 1999, would perform abortions. When the announcement went out that a clinic set to open in Bryan would perform abortions, a Texas A&M student named Lauren heard about it and thought, *I have to do something.* So she called a community-wide meeting to see if others felt the same way. The media got wind of it and provided coverage of the plans for the meeting, so attendance that night was substantial—in fact, four hundred people from sixty churches were represented at that meeting.

There was strong support at the meeting for creating a group to coordinate opposition not just to abortion, but to the opening of a clinic in Bryan where it would be performed. So a board was put together, and Lauren was chosen to head up the organization.

The name chosen for this new nonprofit was Coalition for Life.

That's right. Coalition for Life, the organization that has inspired the formation of similar groups in many cities across the United States, started right here in Bryan, Texas, as a result of the Planned Parenthood clinic where I had been director.

That happened before my time, of course. When Lauren stepped down as director because she married and was starting a family, David Bereit, who had been on the board, was asked to become director. He had only a small staff and little money coming in. Even so, he saw potential in two of his volunteers, a married couple—Shawn and Marilisa Carney. Marilisa had just graduated from college; Shawn was a junior.

One day when Shawn came to pick up Marilisa from her job at Coalition for Life, David asked him to come into one of the back rooms. "I can't offer you anything to eat or drink," David said with a mischievous grin on his face, "because we can't afford anything. So do you mind if we just sit here and play with the leftover ketchup packets while we chat?"

David asked Shawn an age-old question that day: what do you plan to do with your life? Shawn explained that he intended to study law and that he and Marilisa were planning on leaving soon for Notre Dame where Shawn would do just that.

David said, "Here's my problem. I can't afford to pay the staff I have. I need somebody who's willing and able to visit potential donors, orchestrate some fund-raising, and bring in some financial support. I know you're still in school—how about coming on with me part-time now, full-time after you graduate? Can you put off your law-school plans for a while?"

Shawn and Marilisa agreed that the cause was worth it. Marilisa came on full-time and Shawn part-time. And you know when that was? August 2001—exactly one month before my first day as a student volunteer at the clinic. Shawn and I began our work on opposite sides of the fence within thirty days of one another.

Just three years later, from September 1 to October 10, 2004, Coalition for Life conducted its first 40 Days for Life campaign—in Bryan, Texas, right outside the clinic where I worked! It was one of the hottest Septembers in recent memory, and it was right in the middle of a "love bug" infestation (if you're from the South, you'll know all about these annoying black-and-red flying insects). I was a student intern at the clinic by then, but I had no idea this was the first time this campaign had happened anywhere in the country. I figured pro-lifers in other states had done it before. But not so. The Bryan Coalition team thought the idea up themselves. And they prayed.

Forty days straight, twenty-four hours a day, there was always someone praying at the fence that surrounded my Planned Parenthood clinic. And as a result of an intensive door-to-door campaign, Coalition for Life had lined up a prayer support network not just at the fence but throughout the city for those forty days.

I sometimes joke that I know more about 40 Days for Life than anyone—because I've experienced it from both sides of the fence!

Over the next couple of years, David Bereit was asked to speak and assist around the country as other cities heard of the campaign this small yet mighty pro-life group in Bryan, Texas, had conducted around its Planned Parenthood clinic. Those cities wanted a 40 Days for Life campaign of their own, and six other cities soon followed with their own campaigns.

In 2004, during the first 40 Days for Life campaign, David took Marilisa and Shawn out to Subway to break the news. He'd been asked to move to D.C. to take a national pro-life leadership role. But he would agree to do so only if the Carneys would agree to take over Coalition for Life, with Marilisa as executive director. They agreed, and David left for D.C. About a year later, with a young child at home, Marilisa stepped down, and the board asked Shawn to take over as executive director. Oddly enough, this was about the same time that I took the position as director of the Planned Parenthood clinic. Our parts in this story seem to follow parallel paths.

In 2007 David and Shawn, with no money, took a leap of faith and officially launched 40 Days for Life beyond Bryan, Texas. Their goal was to have fifteen to twenty cities participate simultaneously in forty days of prayer and fasting, peaceful vigils outside abortion facilities, and grassroots community outreach. They had no idea what the reaction would be from the rest of the country, and God dramatically exceeded their expectations when eighty-nine cities in thirty-three states signed up and participated in the first national 40 Days for Life campaign that fall. The 40 Days for Life movement was off and running. By 2009, over 300,000 people had participated in campaigns conducted in hundreds of cities across all fifty states and numerous other countries including Canada, Denmark, Australia, and Northern Ireland.

Local campaign leaders and volunteers discovered the same thing that had happened in Bryan, Texas—people of faith and conscience wanted to do something on a local level to help save lives, and 40 Days for Life gave them the opportunity to do just that. As the reports of more than 2,800 lives saved by campaigns poured in from across the country, more volunteers were motivated to hold 40 Days campaigns, and thousands of new people were attracted to join the movement. In fact, over 30 percent of the people who get involved in 40 Days for Life have never participated in any pro-life activity before.

David and Shawn still run 40 Days for Life from their laptops and cell phones, and they personally train the local campaign leaders through online webcasts and teleconferences. They have visited over 300 cities to speak at vigils and encourage local volunteers, and now, as the former director of the abortion facility outside of which this campaign started, I am also a frequent speaker at 40 Days for Life events.

For the most part, media coverage of these events has been widespread and fair, even though there has been little in the way of major national exposure—it's usually the local affiliates that provide the coverage, not the national, prime-time broadcasts. We've had fair media coverage in part because we work hard to make sure all volunteers understand that this is not the time for them to wave their placards, shout insults, or be obnoxious or confrontational.

We are there to stand and pray.

We are there to bear witness to what we know, to what we've already experienced ourselves.

We are there to love and befriend and pray for the clients who enter abortion clinics and the workers who staff them.

Just as I was prayed for, loved, and befriended.

It was a few days after my hearing that I sat at the Coalition for Life house with Shawn, Bobby, Heather, and Karen, as they filled me in on all this history. As the story unfolded, I began to sense the implications of what they were telling me, and a feeling of holy awe began to glow inside me.

"Abby," Shawn said, his eyes deadly serious, "I have to confess that sometimes, in the midst of all the hours and effort, in the face of empty bank accounts and tensions with militant pro-lifers and pro-choicers at each other's throats, in the face of watching women enter that building with apprehension lining their faces and then exiting hours later with grief etched in their countenance, sometimes, Abby, I'd wonder if we were doing any good at all.

"We'd have a few 'saves' at the fence, and whenever we would, we celebrated and sang God's praises. But more often than not, Abby, we prayed and prayed and saw no changes. Women and clinic staff came and went. Babies died. Families were torn apart. But you were a constant, Abby. You'd been there since the beginning for me. I remember how Marilisa talked to you on your very first day. She liked you. And she prayed for you by name. And Elizabeth—she was so sure you would respond to her friendship. She'd tell me, 'Abby is different from many of the executives. She really cares about those women and believes she is helping them. One day, she'll see the truth.' I wanted to believe her, but months turned to years, and there you remained."

Shawn sighed and went quiet for a moment. Then he went on.

"Abby, this year as the 40 Days for Life campaign got started, I was tired. I was beginning to believe our detractors—that abortion was here to stay, that nothing we were doing was making a difference. I was weary, Abby, and beginning to wonder if ours was a lost cause.

And then you showed up at our back door. Right in the midst of the 40 Days for Life campaign."

I tried to swallow the lump in my throat. I'd had no idea Shawn had been discouraged. And I had not realized until that very moment that my conversion was the result of years of prayers over my clinic.

"What got you so invested at Coalition?" I asked him. "I mean, I know about you and Marilisa, but what was it that kept you here?"

He smiled. "The very first time, I came because Marilisa wanted me to. I stood outside the fence but didn't really want to look. I felt so awkward. But then a woman came out of the clinic, and I looked up and our eyes met. And she just kind of looked at me in utter despair and sadness, and I knew we were both sharing this moment, both knowing she had just aborted her child. Her eyes were saying, 'I know what I've just done, it's too late now, and I'm going to carry this the rest of my life.' I remember feeling hopeless but deciding that if I could help just one woman not make that same mistake, I wanted to. And that desire drew me back.

"After that first encounter, abortion was no longer a political issue or a point in some candidate's debate. The distance was removed. I'd witnessed it—helplessly yet hopefully—this terrible, sobering sharing of the decision between life and death. And I truly believed that by being present I could offer a last chance for life to the mother and the baby."

Shawn looked at me then and our eyes locked.

"Abby, remember the day in the parking lot, after I took you to meet Dr. Robinson, when you told me you were going to resign because it was the right thing to do?"

"Of course I remember! I could never forget that—and I thought you were going to burst from joy!"

"At that moment, Abby, at that very moment, I knew that you had been God's plan all along. The whole history of the Coalition for Life flashed through my mind. I thought of a young student hearing on that newscast in 1998 that this clinic was going to open and calling a prayer meeting. She didn't know she was starting a global movement. She was just showing up for God because He called her.

I thought of David Bereit praying his heart out for this place and convincing me to give up law school to take over for him. David didn't have two nickels to rub together, but he prayed. And he showed up. I thought of the day we came up with the forty-day vigil idea and how we prayed so hard that God would change lives through it. And I remembered Marilisa and Elizabeth, and how they both just loved you and never stopped hoping. Abby, all those prayers went up, and God answered those prayers through your story. He knew all along that from this very clinic He would call out Abby Johnson, director of a Planned Parenthood clinic, and hand her a platform to tell the world the truth. And He has, Abby. He has done just that."

And now you know the story too.

As I tell my part of the story, I am joining in the legacy of prayer begun in Bryan, Texas. Every time I stand in front of a microphone or sit in a circle of women or speak words of truth through a fence in some little town in this big country, I am praying for the women and men whom God is going to touch next, the lives He will save, the people He will use.

I will share just one more story, just one of many, but one that makes it all worthwhile for me—the anguish I felt on the day of the ultrasound-guided abortion in September 2009, the anxiety of having to go into court to defend myself, the pain of losing friends and fellowship because they don't support my change from pro-choice to pro-life. All painful memories and all worth it to bring about experiences like this one.

In the spring of 2010, I was praying and standing vigil along-side other people praying outside the fence at the Bryan Planned Parenthood clinic. When the cars of women coming for services at the clinic pulled up, we did what we usually do: Still outside the fence, we walk as near to those women as we can get. Even as they are escorted into the clinic by a Planned Parenthood volunteer, we explain what we can offer them.

It isn't unusual for those women to look ill at ease, and on this day I noticed one woman in particular who looked downright fright-ened. "Hi," I called to her, as the Planned Parenthood volunteer who'd met her at her car cast an unfriendly look my way. "My name is Abby Johnson and I used to be the director of this clinic—that's right, the Planned Parenthood clinic you're heading into right now."

The woman looked at me with confusion.

"I'd just like you to know that there are lots of options available to you right now. Abortion isn't the only one. And at the Coalition for Life office right down the street, we'd be happy to sit with you and help you sort through all those options and how they might affect you. No charge! I hope you have a wonderful day!"

They had arrived at the front door of the clinic by that time, and the troubled woman looked back at me over her shoulder as the escort ushered her through the door. The door shut behind them.

I continued to pray, this time praying specifically for that woman, for her clarity of mind, for the words I'd spoken to bear fruit in her.

Fifteen minutes later she walked back out, still looking trou-bled. She exited the fence, looked around, spotted me, and walked toward me with purpose, crossing through the gate to my side of the fence. "You were the director here at Planned Parenthood?"

I nodded.

"And now you're working with this other group outside the fence?"

I nodded and smiled. It did seem like a strange journey, didn't it?

"Can we go back to your office?" she asked. "I'd like to hear both sides."

I laughed and put my arm around her shoulder, turning her toward Coalition for Life. "Both sides I can handle. I've seen them both."

As we walked, I asked her, "So what's your situation?"

"Well, I went for a checkup. They told me I'm eighteen weeks pregnant."

"Is that what they gave you?" I asked, pointing to the brochure in her hand. I recognized it as a flyer from the National Abortion Federation. On the front was a sticky note with their 1-800 hotline, which refers callers to clinics that do late-term abortions.

"Yes." She looked down.

"Is that what you are going to do?" I asked her gently.

"I already have six children," she answered. "How can I have another baby?"

I smiled. "You just called this newest child a baby, so I can see you already know you're his or her mother."

She smiled in acknowledgment.

"We can help you," I told her. By now we'd arrived at the Coalition for Life house. I invited her into the same room where I'd been invited. One of our counselors joined us, and within thirty minutes she was connected to a clinic offering a free ultrasound and prenatal and birthing care; a source of free diapers for a year; coupons for food for herself and her children; and a group that would provide her with a free car seat and furniture for the baby.

"I'll walk you back to your car," I offered, and we strolled back to the Planned Parenthood clinic, where we hugged before she climbed into her car and waved good-bye.

Another car pulled into the lot, and a new Planned Parenthood volunteer escort, one I hadn't seen before, stepped out of the clinic to greet the client.

"Hi," I called. "I'm Abby. I just want you to know we are here to help in any way we can."

The Planned Parenthood escort looked at me quizzically, and I smiled back.

I wonder what her story is, and what God is going to do in her life.

ACKNOWLEDGMENTS

There are so many people I need to thank. I could write a book on how many people have helped me through this journey. I want to start off by thanking my parents. You are responsible for this. Sometimes "this" may not be something you want to take credit for, but in this case, I hope I have made you proud.

None of this would be possible without the unwavering strength of my husband, Doug. Every girl dreams of "having it all." I know that I have found that in you. You are definitely the most patient man in the world; I know that has been tested while married to me! But I am so thankful that you continue to be patient with me. Where I fail, you exceed by leaps and bounds. Thank you for always helping me keep our family close to my heart even when I am away. Also, thank you to Doug's best friends, Daniel and Ben. It is always good to have people to help us keep our sanity. You have been such an encouragement to Doug and to me.

Shawn, there are really no words to express my gratitude to you and your family. During the most difficult time in my life, you were my rock—always steady handed, always there to make me laugh. It makes me chuckle to think that we were once opposed to each other. It feels like we have been partners in this movement for a lifetime. I can't wait to see what the future holds for both of us.

I guess I could thank David for this whole 40 Days for Life movement, but even that wouldn't be enough. David, your mentorship and friendship mean more than I can express. You took me into your "family" when I felt so lost and deserted and helped me feel like I belonged again. Your encouragement and support have been some of the greatest gifts I have received. Your whole family is such a blessing to me and my family.

I, of course, have to thank everyone involved with the Brazos Valley Coalition for Life. Without all of you, I wouldn't be here today. It is your faithfulness, your perseverance that help women face the truth of abortion every day. I especially want to thank Bobby, Heather, and Karen. You guys supported me and listened to me when I thought my world was falling apart. You have been on this ride with me and have experienced all the ups and downs. You have prayed with me, you have cried with me, you have laughed with me. You are not just my friends, you are my heroes. I thank God every day that He put you in my life.

Marcel and Heather, you have been my spiritual gurus! You guys have kept me focused on Christ and His will for my life. You have kept me grounded, and you continue to help me draw closer and closer to Him every day. Thank you so much for all of your guidance.

Even though I lost many friends throughout this journey, some remained. Also, many more were gained. Three "old" friends who have always stuck by me deserve a *big* thanks. Michelle, Amy, and Gabe, you know all of the ugly and bad about me but you love me anyway. That is real friendship. You have been there for me during the darkest and brightest times of my life. I can never repay you for your endless support, but I will spend every day trying my best. I love you guys so much. And to one of my "new" friends, Claire. I am so thankful that God has brought you into my life. You have shown me the power of redemption and forgiveness through your life. Your friendship is one of the greatest blessings I have received.

I would be remiss if I didn't give a thank-you to my "friend from the fence," Elizabeth. One of the coolest moments of the past year for me was celebrating your birthday with you. I just had to stand there for a moment to really take in the enormity of that event. You, the sidewalk counselor who befriended me several years ago, and me, the former Planned Parenthood worker, celebrating your birth together. You are a treasure to me. Your friendship, your advice, your jokes, everything . . . all are priceless. You are my angel on earth.

Jeff, I can't think of anyone who could have better represented me in court against Planned Parenthood. It's funny to say it, but I think we actually had a good time! You and Shawn did such an amazing job of protecting me during that time. I felt so vulnerable, but you were always so confident. Sorry about *O'Reilly*! Maybe next time!

To the folks at Ambassador Agency, Gloria, Wes, Emily, and Maria. You are my natural stress relievers. You keep my head on straight. I couldn't do any of this without you; and I don't just mean the planning, but also your friendship and guidance. I couldn't work with a better team . . . everyone should be so lucky.

I may be biased, but I believe I have the very best family in the whole world. Thank you all for always supporting me and loving me throughout my life. Also, thanks to Doug's family. Thank you for allowing him to marry a kooky liberal. I think I finally have my act together! I love you all so very much!

Cindy, my incredible literary partner. How could I have gotten through this process without you? Clearly, our partnership was one initiated by God. No one else could have told this story in a more powerful and truthful way. You captured my voice in every sentence. You are such a blessing to me. I look forward to working with you many more times in the future.

Last but definitely not least, I want to thank my former coworkers from Planned Parenthood. Even though many of our lives have gone in different directions, I value the relationships that we established for so many years. So many of you helped shape who I am today. I appreciate all of you and treasure the many wonderful memories we shared together. I pray that one day I will be able to reconnect with some of you. You all mean so much to me and are still a huge part of my life and my heart. I hope that one day we will be standing together again, but this time on this side of the "fence."

ENDNOTES

1 Planned Parenthood affiliates continue to make this assertion in some of their literature, such as the "Planned Parenthood and Parental Notification" statement, which says, "Planned Parenthood believes that the best way to make abortion rare is to make sure women, families and teens have access to confidential and affordable reproductive health care services." See http://www.plannedparenthood.org/rocky-mountains/planned-parenthood-parental-notification-10565.htm (accessed September 4, 2010). When reacting to the 40 Days for Life campaign in 2010, Planned Parenthood Gulf Coast released this statement: "Planned Parenthood does more than any other organization to prevent unintended pregnancies and the need for abortion." See Stephanie Palmer, "'Forty Days for Life' Campaign Kicks Off," KBTX.com, September 21, 2010, http://www.kbtx.com/local/headlines/103489104.html (accessed September 22, 2010).

2 These general figures are confirmed by Rachel K. Jones, Jacqueline E. Darroch, and Stanley K. Henshaw, "Patterns in the Socioeconomic Characteristics of Women Obtaining Abortions in 2000–2001," *Perspectives on Sexual and Reproductive Health* 34, no. 5, September/October 2002, http://www.guttmacher.org/pubs/journals/3422602.html.

3 Just after assuming her post in 2006, the current president of Planned Parenthood Federation of America told the *New York Times*, "No one does more to reduce the need for abortions in this country than Planned Parenthood." Robin Finn, "Anti-Abortion Advocates? Bring 'Em On, Texan Says," New York Times, March 10, 2006, http://www.nytimes.com/2006/03/10/nyregion/10lives.html?_r=1 (accessed October 1, 2010).

4 Rachel K. Jones, Lawrence B. Finer, and Susheela Singh, "Characteristics of U.S. Abortion Patients, 2008," Guttmacher Institute, May 2010, http://www.guttmacher.org/pubs/US-Abortion-Patients.pdf (accessed September 22, 2010).

5 In 2010, Planned Parenthood of Houston and Southeast Texas and Planned Parenthood of Louisiana and the Mississippi Delta became known as Planned Parenthood Gulf Coast. Though they had been working as merged affiliates for about five years, they held on to their respective names until September 1, 2010. See http://www.plannedparenthood.org/gulf-coast/who-we-are-33227.htm.

6 Potential serious side effects of these drugs are well established. See, for example, U.S. Food and Drug Administration, "Medication Guide: Mifeprex," revised July 19, 2005, http://www.fda.gov/downloads/Drugs/DrugSafety/ucm088643.pdf and National Abortion Federation, "Facts about Mifepristone (RU-486)," updated February 2008, http://www.prochoice.org/pubs_research/publications/downloads/about_abortion/facts_about_mifepristone.pdf (accessed September 29, 2010).

7 The affiliate's 2008–2009 annual report acknowledges that the hurricanes, sluggish economy, and other financial challenges had made the year a difficult one: "Uncertain economic times called for an affiliate-wide response. We were able to close our fiscal year on a positive note due to across the board expense cuts, a reduction in force and a freeze on employee merit increases." See Planned Parenthood of Houston and Southeast Texas, "Annual Report 2008–2009," http://www.plannedparenthood.org/gulf-coast/images/Gulf-Coast/AR_2008-2009.pdf.

8 Cindy Horswell, "Anti-Abortion Protestors Target Planned Parenthood," January 18, 2010, *Houston Chronicle*, http://www.chron.com/disp/story.mpl/health/6821521.html; Cindy George, "Planned Parenthood Debuts New Building," May 20, 2010, *Houston Chronicle*, http://www.chron.com/disp/story.mpl/metropolitan/7015381.html.

9 In its 2008–2009 Annual Report, Planned Parenthood of Southeast Texas and Houston refers to a cutback in these funds, saying "And despite lower allocations of Federal family planning Title XX funds to our health centers in Texas, more than 52% of our visits were provided at low or no cost to our clients."

10 Increasing the number of abortions at our clinic would simply reflect the overall rise in the number of abortions performed by Planned Parenthood Federation of America over the past several years: There were 264,943 abortions performed in 2005; 289,750 in 2006; 305,310 in 2007; and 324,008 in 2008, the latest year for which figures are available. These statistics come from Planned Parenthood Federation of America's 2006–2007 and 2007–2008 Annual Reports, as well as Planned Parenthood Federation of America, "Planned Parenthood Services," fact sheet, September 2010, http://www.plannedparenthood.org/files/PPFA/fact_ppservices_2010-09-03.pdf.

11 *The Book of Common Prayer, According to the Use of The Episcopal Church* (New York: Church Publishing Incorporated, 1979), 355.

12 Ibid., 137, 266, 657; taken from Psalm 51:10, KJV.

13 For an interesting look at the way Planned Parenthood often thinks like a business, see Stephanie Simon, "Extending the Brand: Planned Parenthood Hits Suburbia," Wall Street Journal, June 23, 2008, http://online.wsj.com/article_email/SB121417762585295459-lMyQjAxMDI4MTIoMzEyNzM3Wj.html (accessed October 1, 2010).

14 See, for example, Planned Parenthood Action Center, "Fighting Anti-Choice Extremism," http://www.plannedparenthoodaction.org/positions/opposing-attacks-womens-health-785.htm (accessed October 4, 2010).

15 Ashlea Sigman, "Planned Parenthood Director Leaves, Has Change of Heart," KBTX.com, November 1, 2009, http://www.kbtx.com/home/headlines/68441827.html.
16 *The Book of Common Prayer,* 454–455.
17 Tracy Clark-Flory, "The Conversion of a Pro-Choice Warrior," *Broadsheet,* Salon Media Group, November 3, 2009, http://www.salon.com/life/broadsheet/feature/2009/11/03/planned_parenthood (accessed September 4, 2010).
18 Anne-Marie Dorning, "Planned Parenthood Clinic Director Joins Anti-Abortion Group," ABCNews.com, November 5, 2009, http://abcnews.go.com/Health/MindMoodNews/planned-parenthood-clinic-director-joins-anti-abortion-group/story?id=8999720 (accessed September 22, 2010).
19 Dialogue taken from *Planned Parenthood of Houston and Southeast Texas, Inc. and Planned Parenthood of Southeast Texas Surgical and Comprehensive Health and Services, Inc. v. Abby Johnson and the Brazos Valley Coalition for Life*, which was heard in the Brazos County, Texas, 85th Judicial District on November 10, 2009. The actual names of Planned Parenthood staff have been replaced with the pseudonyms used throughout the book. Some punctuation has been tweaked for clarity and consistency.
20 Matthew Watkins, "Planned Parenthood Denied Injunction," *Bryan-College Station Eagle,* November 11, 2009, http://www.theeagle.com/local/Planned-Parenthood-denied-injunction (accessed September 4, 2010).

Find out the latest news about *Unplanned* at www.unplannedthebook.com.

You can also visit Abby's personal website at www.abbyjohnson.org for more resources, including updates from Abby and ways to get involved in helping women who face crisis pregnancies.

ABOUT THE AUTHORS

Abby Johnson holds a B.S. in psychology from Texas A&M University and an M.A. in counseling from Sam Houston State University. She was hired by Planned Parenthood in 2005 and progressed to the position of community services director and health educator, where she served as liaison between the community and Planned Parenthood as media correspondent. Later promoted to health center director, Johnson ran both the family planning and abortion programs. In 2009 she left Planned Parenthood and joined the local Coalition for Life as a volunteer. Johnson now serves as chief research strategist for Live Action and works on projects with the national 40 Days for Life campaign. She and her husband, Doug, have a young daughter and live in Texas.

Cindy Lambert, vice president and associate publisher at Zondervan, is a veteran of the bookselling industry. For nearly two decades she owned an award-winning bookstore before expanding into leadership roles in distribution, editorial, and publishing in such companies as Ingram, Simon & Schuster, and Zondervan. As a speaker Cindy has addressed audiences in publishing and bookselling conferences as well as churches and retreats. She and her husband, Dave, have six children and seven grandchildren, and live in Michigan.

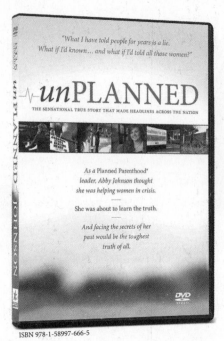

Online Discussion *guide*

TAKE *your* TYNDALE READING EXPERIENCE *to the* NEXT LEVEL

A FREE discussion guide for this book is available at bookclubhub.net, perfect for sparking conversations in your book group or for digging deeper into the text on your own.

www.bookclubhub.net

You'll also find free discussion guides for other Tyndale books, e-newsletters, e-mail devotionals, virtual book tours, and more!

CP0071

LIFE-AFFIRMING *programs at Focus on the Family*

Lee and Cort King

Helping women make informed choices

"I didn't think just seeing a picture would impact me at all. I just knew that I needed an ultrasound if I was going to have an abortion. I had no idea the bond that I would feel with my baby. Seeing him on ultrasound made me look at my pregnancy in a different way. I mostly remember seeing his teeny, tiny heart beating so fast. He was real and he was in *me*! Without the ultrasound, I'm not sure that I'd have my beautiful baby boy."

—*Lee King, Memphis, Tennessee*

In 2004, Focus on the Family launched the Option Ultrasound™ Program, a groundbreaking initiative providing grants for ultrasound machines and sonography training to pregnancy medical clinics across the country. As a result, we estimate that as of 2010 nearly 90,000 mothers like Lee have chosen life for their babies.

To read more stories of moms impacted by Option Ultrasound and to find out how you can help, visit www.heartlink.org.

ADVOCATE *for the* NEEDS *of women & children.*

Model used for illustrative purposes only.

Every child deserves to know the love of a forever family.

Here's how the Focus on the Family Adoption & Orphan Care Initiative is helping to make that happen.

Wait No More®: Finding Families for Waiting Kids
Given the number of churches throughout the U.S., every waiting child in U.S. foster care could have a family today if less than one family per church opened their home and hearts. Through Wait No More events, Focus on the Family is working collaboratively with church and state, county, and adoption agency leaders to raise awareness and recruit adoptive families for waiting children and youth.

Cry of the Orphan™
Working in collaboration with Hope for Orphans® (a ministry of FamilyLife®) and Show Hope® (founded by Steven Curtis and Mary Beth Chapman), Focus on the Family conducts national Cry of the Orphan campaigns to raise awareness of the plight of orphans around the world and to connect people with organizations that help orphans.

Post-Placement Resources and Support
Focus on the Family develops and distributes resources that are relevant to the unique struggles of adoptive families. These resources also provide practical ways churches and individuals can support the adoptive families in their communities. In addition, Focus on the Family is working on ways to increase access to adoption-competent Christian counselors throughout the country.

For more information, visit www.iCareAboutOrphans.org.

FocusOnTheFamily.com
800-A-Family (232-6459)

CP0450